THE MOTIVATION CODE

COMPLETE HYPNOTHERAPY PROGRAM FOR
MOTIVATION - INCLUDES 2.5 HRS OF AUDIO
HYPNOSIS DOWNLOADS

RICK SMITH - HPD DHYP

The Legal Bit...

I am a Certified Clinical Hypnotherapist. I am not a doctor or licensed medical practitioner, and I do not offer medical advice or diagnosis.

You're free to use hypnosis as you see fit, however if you have any doubts concerning it's efficacy in your case, you should seek guidance from a qualified medical practitioner.

Please do not play hypnosis recordings whilst driving or operating machinery.

Headphones or earbuds are recommended for privacy and effectiveness, when playing the hypnosis recordings.

CONTENTS

ABOUT THE AUTHOR

Rick Smith graduated as a Certified Clinical Hypnotherapist in London in 2006, and holds the NCH Hypnotherapist Practitioner Diploma from the Surrey Institute of
Clinical Hypnotherapy.

His online practice ricksmithhypnosis.com offers a
variety of audio hypnosis programs covering areas such

as Anxiety, Confidence, Workplace Stress, Procrastination, Weight Loss, and Health & Fitness.

Rick's *How to Master Self-Hypnosis in a Weekend* has been a regular Amazon bestseller since it's publication in 2013.

Other Rick Smith Hypnosis Books & Programs in this series are available from Amazon or as audiobook versions from www.ricksmithhypnosis.com

- Cool, Calm, Confident You
- Do It Now - Crush Procrastination
- The Determination Diet
- Active Energy Now - Exercise Motivation
- Sleep Fast, Sleep Deep, Sleep Now
- Crush Stress Now
- Master Self-Hypnosis in a Weekend
- The Motivation Code
- An Ocean of Calm - Ultimate Tranquility
- Breaking The Ice - Social Anxiety & Shyness
- Sugar Free - Crush Your Sugar Addiction
- Stop Hating Your Job - Banish Workplace Stress
- Own The Stage - Presentation & Performance Confidence

Why not join me on Facebook...

https://www.facebook.com/ricksmithhypnosis/

Ways To Use This Book

This book includes several full-length hypnosis sessions which are the key elements of the program. How you use these is up to you.

You can read them and record them for yourself. Hardly anyone does this, because...

You can download my professionally recorded sessions free of charge, and play them back on your phone, tablet, or computer. You'll find the full instructions in Chapter 4.

The first part of the book will explain how the process works, and it'll help with your hypnosis preparation and set-up. Even thought the recordings work fine on their own, I recommend you read this part first.

Elsewhere in the book, we'll explore the various subjects in more detail, however it's not necessary for you to read these sections for the program to be effective.

Simply relax, and trust the process.

 facebook.com/ricksmithhypnosis

1

WELCOME TO THE PROGRAM

So, what's holding you back?

WHATEVER HAPPENED to your easy life?

These days, there's so much to do. It saps your energy and your focus. Some days you just can't be bothered...

Need a little help to get moving?

Your *logical* brain knows what you need to do, and when and how to do it. But your *emotional* brain is pulling you backwards, acting like a hacker, sending you false code -

- *"Don't start that task because we might fail, and we know how that feels!"*

• *"It's so cosy here on the sofa, we can paint the fence some other time!"*

• *"We don't need a promotion, who wants to hustle that hard?"*

So you languish in your comfort zone, fooling yourself that this is the life you want, when you're actually feeling guilty, embarrassed, or ashamed because you know it's not the life you really need.

You should be *doing something.*

Time to change the code

Your demotivation may be caused or triggered by external events.

Maybe you just don't feel appreciated or rewarded; this is not what you signed up for.

Alternately, it may be an ingrained pattern of behaviour caused by adolescent experiences or past shortfalls - you feel destined to under-perform, so you continually set yourself up that way.

When you're demotivated like this, life can be pretty joyless.

You can be better.

You have the resources, now here's the system.

Your situation is caused by your emotional *bad code,* causing you to behave sub-optimally, and it's holding you back from achieving your potential.

Hypnosis a proven, successful method of helping people make the necessary and appropriate changes - to their mindset, their habits, and their schedules - to find the motivation they seek.

Whatever you've tried before probably hasn't worked, at least not for very long.

Hypnosis is different. In the three sessions of *The Motivation Code,* we'll hunt down that broken code, and replace it with new, effective programming that will fire your positive, energetic *"Let's Get This Done"* response instead of your old *"Let's Not Bother Today"* submission. You'll regain control over what you do, when you do it, and the benefits you receive.

And you'll feel a whole lot better than you do right now!

THIS BOOK IS an extended version of my original audio download program. It includes:

- An overview of this program, the hypnosis methods we'll be using, and full instructions to prepare you for hypnosis

- My two-part thirty-minute hypnosis training and conditioning audio program, to get you used to going in and out of hypnosis, smoothly and easily. If you're already used to hypnosis, or you've completed any of my other programs, you can skim through this section, or skip it altogether.

- Three targeted hypnotherapy sessions to directly address the key components of your motivation, totalling around two hours of professionally recorded hypnotherapy.

You can download or stream the recorded sessions, free for life, by following the simple instructions in Chapter 4.

Never play these recordings whilst driving or operating any kind of machinery. Please be responsible (I know you are).

How I Know This Works

There's a lot of snake-oil out there in the hypnosis industry, so why should you trust me?

Well, you already know that I'm certified (that's the big-shot letters after my name) so I'm ethically bound to provide my best professional efforts to my clients.

But if you need more: Here's a screenshot from my online store, which sells these programs in audio download format. As you can see, 42% of my sales are to returning customers (as of October 2018).

So I guess it works!

Recordings vs. Face-to-Face Hypnotherapy

So, how does recorded hypnotherapy compare to a visit to the hypnotherapist's office?

Does this way work the same?

Well, it's not exactly the same, primarily because some conventional - *analytical* - hypnotherapy techniques require two-way communication between therapist and client, which is clearly impractical for us.

However, that doesn't mean it's less effective. Far from it!

Imagine this;

- You book an appointment with your nearest hypnotherapist, probably a few days in advance.
- For days you worry about the visit; *will it work, will I like the therapist, can I afford the cost, can I get time off?*
- The day arrives, and you're already anxious about the journey, apprehensive of meeting a stranger, unhappy about the weather, and concerned about your work or family situation.
- You struggle downtown, with all the inconvenience and cost, and finally arrive, unsettled and stressed, for your session.
- You now put yourself in the hands of a complete stranger, and spend the first half of the session wondering if it's working.
- By the time you're relaxed, it's over, and you have

to battle your way back home, maybe more than a hundred pounds or dollars lighter.

- Once you get home, you try to replicate what the therapist taught you, but half of it's just a distant memory.

You may give up completely. Your problem wasn't solved.

The Alternative;

- You decide to try hypnotherapy to boost your Motivation.
- You buy, beg, borrow or steal a copy of *The Motivation Code* which will never be more than seven pounds / ten dollars.
- You find a quiet, comfortable space at home, put on your headphones, and listen to the sessions, which I've specifically created and adapted to work effectively in a *one-way* environment.
- You practice your new skills straight away, and repeat your hypnosis sessions whenever necessary, anytime, anywhere.

Now, how's that *not* going to work better?

Of course, there are many complex conditions which can't readily be adapted for audio hypnotherapy, and which really do benefit from the live clinical experience. That's why I don't publish programs about depression, addiction (except sugar addiction!) or grief.

Pretty much everything else works just fine!

2

HOW THIS WORKS

How Does It Work?

FORMS OF HYPNOSIS have been a regular feature of ancient civilisations, some of whose rituals survive to this day. Shaman, Faith Healers, Cults and Religions have used and continue to use forms of hypnosis with their followers. Chanting, music and singing, sermonising, meditation, and even the use of psychoactive substances, natural and unnatural, are used to induce transient states in their followers.

Hypnotherapy is the practice of inducing this *trance state* in an individual (that's the *hypno* part) which suppresses your conscious critical faculty and enables carefully-crafted, congruent verbal communication to pass directly through the usual filters, to communicate with parts of the mind that are usually closed off to direct access - the subconscious - where habits and behaviours are stored and operated.

Everyday things like walking, talking, and eating are down there, as well as more complex skills that we acquire through our lives, like driving or tightrope walking!

Your subconscious mind is responsible for your automatic responses; how you act or behave in a specific situation. Such responses are learned over time, and sometimes, if some distorted information has been fed in - usually quite early in your life - your response to certain situations may be off-centre, causing you problems.

That's where the *therapy* part comes in. Whilst you're suspended in that open-minded, accepting state, the hypnotherapist will use his skills to change or adapt replace your habits and behaviour, over-writing your old, troublesome beliefs and responses with more appropriate new ones.

When hypnotised, you're able to accept these new 'machine instructions' unquestioningly, because the skilled therapist will demonstrate to you that your new way of doing things is more beneficial, and serves you better, than your old way.

As this is the primary directive of your automated subconscious – to protect you and ensure you thrive – it's readily accepted, and with application and repetition, your new habits are embedded for good.

The Stages

Hypnotherapy has several stages. Each one segues directly into the next, ensuring that the whole process is smooth and relaxed, with no bumps in the road.

1. Preamble

In the first stage, you're encouraged to find a comfortable position, and simply listen to an introduction. This preamble is intended to start the ball rolling, and focus you on the subject or issue you're going to be working on in hypnosis. Although this is not strictly part of the trance, it's a very important component of the process, and should ever be skipped.

2. Induction

At the appropriate moment, you'll be encouraged to close your eyes and begin the induction process. In this phase, the therapist uses a range of relaxation, visualisation, and imagination techniques to guide your descent to an adequate depth of trance for the work to begin.

There are many different forms of induction, some fast, some not so much.

In my courses, I start off using a specially modified medium-length and highly effective induction – the *Dave Elman Induction* – which is one of the most popular amongst experienced hypnotherapists.

In subsequent sessions, I introduce shorter, more rapid inductions, once you, the client, are conditioned to going easily into hypnosis.

3. The 'Work'

Once you are sufficiently deep in the hypnotic state, however that comes to you, the work can begin. Depending on the issue, there are a wide variety of 'therapeutic' approaches which can be used.

Here are just a few:

- *Visualisation*
- *Sensory Simulation*
- *Age Regression*
- *Time Compression*
- *Metaphor*
- *Coaching Techniques*
- *Breathing Techniques*
- *Re-Framing*
- *Triggers and Anchors*
- *Self-Hypnosis*
- *Pattern Interruption*
- *Modified Self-Talk*
- *Ego Strengthening*

For my programs, given the obvious limitation of tailoring the approach for each individual client, I have concentrated on using the optimum combination of techniques for these one-way recorded sessions.

We won't be delving into the dark corners of your life (if you have any) looking for eureka moments. You won't be beating your chest or clucking like a chicken either, I'm afraid.

You'll just be focusing on accepting that you need to make a change, and then making it happen, in the most appropriate, beneficial way.

4. The Emerge

Once the work is completed, you'll be gently guided back to a full waking state. You may remember everything, or you may remember nothing at all. As we said in the beginning, everyone experiences it differently, and I'm pleased to report there seems to be no correlation between 'reported' depth of trance and the effectiveness of the program.

5. The Debrief

After the Emerge phase, you'll be invited to review what happened, and the changes you have made. In many cases, I'll be setting you some homework, to practice what you've learned, and help to drive your new habits deeper so they stay strong and permanent.

This real-life work is equally as important as the hypnosis, because regular practice of your new way of doing things reinforces your new synapses, those connections in your brain which carry the messages between its different parts.

This is the science of neuroplasticity, the ability of the brain to rewire itself when required to do so. It works.

The State

So, now you understand how it works, how does it feel? And how will you know when you reach it?

It's practically impossible to describe the sensations of hypnosis to someone who's never experienced it, for two reasons.

- Firstly, because there are many, many different states, often unique to an individual. How someone relaxes and *lets go* is always coloured by their life, situation and environment. Everyone accepts hypnosis in their own unique way.
- Secondly, the state of hypnosis defies words, at least words of sufficient eloquence to describe it adequately. Can you describe how you felt in the last minute before you fell asleep last night?

You'll be familiar with that *in-between state between awake and asleep,* when your mind wanders and you start to dream, sometimes in short flashes, in between the little naps that drift in and out. So if you know how that feels, you'll be close to understanding how hypnosis feels – like hovering in that state, still aware, but otherwise detached from your physical environment.

But you won't have the words to describe it adequately, so there's no need to try.

Just accept it, and enjoy the experience.

Using The Scripts and Recordings

Each of the hypnosis scripts is printed long-hand in this book. If you want to, you can read and record the scripts yourself. Around one-in-fifty of my clients and readers appear to opt for that.

If you want a quicker fix - maybe you prefer not to listen to your own voice - I've recorded them for you, with my (professional hypnotherapist's) voice, and you can download or stream these recordings free of charge for life. The access instructions are in the Chapter 4.

It's easy, I promise.

I recommend you use your smartphone, mp3 player, or tablet computer as the quickest and most convenient method. You can carry the recordings with you, so you can use them anywhere, anytime. I've included instructions about how to do this on Apple and Android devices, and I'm sure if you're a Windows, Sony, or Blackberry user, you'll be able to adapt these instructions for your own device.

If you encounter any issues, please e-mail me at rick@ricksmithhypnosis.com and I'll fix it for you. A few of my Amazon reviewers have complained that they couldn't access the scripts in the past, and punished me with one or two stars. These issues are invariably down to a user's own settings, so if you mail me you'll get a quick solution, and I'll avoid any more negative reviews!

If you don't use a portable device, you can play the recordings from your PC or Mac. Somewhere in the world, somebody's probably listening to them on a cassette player or even an 8-track. Let me know if it's you!

You can download or stream the scripts by clicking the link at the beginning of the next chapter. You'll receive an immediate e-mail with your access details.

The System

Repetition is a key strategy with hypnosis of any kind, and you'll discover lots of opportunities to drop into trance and practice your skills.

Everything you need to know, and everything you need to do, is laid out in sequence. All you need to succeed is to follow the system.

If you enjoy the program and you find it useful, please take a moment to post a review on Amazon. When my first hypnosis audio/book - *How to Master Self-Hypnosis in a Weekend* - was published in 2013, there were maybe twenty books on the subject. Now there are hundreds, and most of them are disappointing, so if you find this book worthwhile, please help others to discover it by reviewing it. Thanks.

Now, just relax and enjoy the ride.

3

THE 'MOTIVATION CODE' APPROACH

Why Hypnosis is your best option…

FIRST OF ALL, I'd like to welcome you to this program, and congratulate you on taking a big, big step towards overcoming your motivation issues, whatever they may be.

You're not alone; Many people suffer all their lives, and never acknowledge that they need help to get on top of the bad habits and feelings of anxiety that come with their lack of motivation.

In the three sessions of *The Motivation Code,* we'll hunt down that broken code, and replace it with new, effective code that will fire your positive, energetic motivation.

- **Session One** focuses on your desires, goals, and objectives, and teaches you define *destinations* and *journeys*. You'll sharpen your long-range focus so that you can start to gain perspective, and control your short-term challenges with micro-planning rituals. Once you rediscover the pleasures of successful outcomes, you'll channel your energy into getting past the hard stuff quickly, without prevarication.

- **Session Two** borrows from the mindsets and rituals of Olympic athletes, to equip you with powerful secret weapons for getting off the start line, executing race strategy, and finishing strongly every time. Distractions fall away when you have just one important job to do!

- **Session Three** reveals choices you hadn't considered, and shows you how to dump your complicated cocktail of negative thinking - *the bad code* - in a vault so secure that it simply won't come back to influence you in the future. Once you're free of your artificial emotional restraints, you'll see the full picture - maybe for the first time - and the immense potential you possess.

Once you have a clear target and a solid plan, and you replace that bad code you don't need any more, you won't recognise the old you.

You'll feel powerful, you'll radiate positive energy, and you'll join the legion of successful, motivated people who know how to use The Motivation Code to get what they want.

Training and Conditioning

As with all my courses and programs, this one will work many times better and faster if you're comfortable going in and out of trance. If you've tried hypnosis or hypnotherapy in the past, and feel that it worked for you, you should be fine.

If this is your first time, I recommend you complete my two short Training and Conditioning recordings before you set to work on your anxiety.

Hypnosis is progressive, and the more often you do it, the faster, smoother, and deeper it becomes. By conditioning yourself with the training sessions, you'll find the therapeutic value of the main recordings will be many times more effective.

The Training and Conditioning recordings come free in your download package, and the transcripts are printed long-hand in Section 1.

When you're ready to begin, make yourself comfortable

and make sure you won't be disturbed. Draw the shades, eliminate any distracting noises, and prepare yourself to be hypnotised.

Each of the recordings has a short introduction, or pre-amble, following which you'll begin the hypnosis.

4

USING THE RECORDINGS

IN THIS CHAPTER, we're going to look at two important practical aspects of this hypnosis program;

- How to access and use the recorded sessions, using your computer, smartphone or tablet,
- Preparing and setting up your ideal hypnosis environment.

The Hard Way - Record It for Yourself

In the next section, the scripts are printed long-hand. You can read and record them yourself, using your smart-phone's Voice Memo or Voice Recorder function (or any other recording device), and then play them back as many times as you need.

If you're using your smartphone as the recording device, the easiest way to record your own voice is to use the microphone attached to your hands-free headphones. This avoids you having to hold the phone and gives you easier access to the controls. You'll be able to pause and re-start the recording as needed.

However, listening to your own voice is not ideal, and you probably don't have experience in reciting hypnosis scripts, which rely for their effectiveness on certain voice techniques.

So, although this is a perfectly practical way to work with the scripts in this book, I seriously recommend you use my pre-recorded versions as explained below. You'll get a better result and it will be much quicker to get started.

The Easy Way - Using My Recordings

All the scripts I used to create these recordings are included in the book. The Training Scripts are at the end of Section 1 , and the Main Scripts are in Section 2.

Many clients buy my hypnotherapy programs as audio-books from my website. The recordings you'll be accessing through this book are the same high-quality audio downloads, and you're free to download or stream them whenever you like.

How to Get the Recordings

The recordings are securely stored on Amazon Web Services (AWS) so that they can be played or downloaded 24/7. I chose AWS to host my recordings (more than 200, at last count) because of their platform's reliability and easy access for you, my client, on any device.

By the way, they're not paying me to say that!

If you experience any difficulties in accessing these recorded sessions, please e-mail me at **helpdesk@rick-smithhypnosis.com** and I will solve it for you.

My hypnosis recordings have been streamed or down-loaded more than 100,000 times, and I receive just one or two help-desk emails in an average week. I've simplified the access process so you should have no issues, but please get in touch if you do.

So, let's get you organised right now:

When you click on this link (or type it into your browser if you're reading the print version) it will open up a little form on your screen. Please enter your first name and your email address (so I know where to send your record-ings) and submit the form.

That's all you need to do.

http://tiny.cc/amzmotv

Within a minute or two, you'll receive an email from **rick@ricksmithhypnosis.com**, containing your access information. Please keep this email safe, so you can access the sessions anytime.

It's not unknown for this first e-mail to go into your junk folder, so please check there first if you don't receive it within three minutes of registering.

The email you receive will direct you to the secure download page for this program. Once there, you'll have two options. You can use either or both:

On Your Phone or Tablet

Each session in the program has a Download button. When you click the button, the track will start to play. Simple!

On Your Computer

You can play the tracks on your computer in exactly the same way, however you can also download them to keep or share.

To do this, start the track using the Download button,

then pause it and right click in the play-bar controls and choose Download.

The individual audio files are MP3's, the same as a song you might download from iTunes or Google Play.

Download the Whole Program

Because the tracks are longer (30-45 minutes each), and there are several tracks in each program, they've been compressed and packaged into what's called a 'Zip' file, to make them easier and faster to deliver by download.

If you opt to download the .zip file, you will get the complete program (it may take a few minutes) on your computer's hard drive. From there, you click on it and it will open and unpack the individual recordings as MP3's.

Once you can see each of the individual tracks, you can simply play each one by clicking on it, or you can transfer the tracks (just like music) to your phone or tablet, using whatever method you would usually use for songs. If you're struggling with this, ask a nearby teenager to help you!

Once you've done that, you can open your music player (such as iTunes) and find the track in the alphabetic list of all your stored music tracks. The artist name is Rick Smith.

If you download it to your 'Downloads' or 'Desktop', you can play the recordings direct, or open iTunes or your preferred music player, and import the file.

You can play it from there, or alternately you might decide to create a new Playlist (perhaps call it 'Hypnosis Sessions') and drag the track into it. Then you'll easily be able to find it, and when you sync to your phone or tablet next time, make sure you add the playlist and you'll be able to find it easily on your device, which is where you really need it to be.

On Your Phone or Tablet

Downloading the whole program's *zip* file to your phone or tablet isn't an option for most people, because these devices don't usually have a file system to open and store the tracks.

So instead, you can access the individual sessions and play (stream) them live, wherever you have Wi-Fi or data available, from the Download Page (see above).

Your *welcome and access email* will show you where to find the recordings, and it's one simple click to start, pause, or stop them at any time.

If you decide to go this way, you can be up and running on your portable device within three minutes of clicking or typing the link below, and you can always go back and download the whole program when you're near your computer.

This means you can access the recordings from anywhere you have data access. Each recorded session is typically 30-40MB (equivalent to 6 - 8 mp3 songs), so please be careful if you have a limited data plan with your phone carrier. Wi-fi, particularly at home, is often free or unlimited, so that's the best and most economical way to access the recordings.

Whenever you use your portable device for playing sessions - which you'll be doing a lot throughout this program - please use headphones or earbuds for privacy. This also helps to block out external noises, which can be a distraction during your hypnosis sessions.

All set? Good. Here's the link that will get you rapid access to the recordings for this program.

http://tiny.cc/amzmotv

And if you hit any snags, email me here:

helpdesk@ricksmithhypnosis.com

By the way, I'm not a corporation with a call centre. There's just me here, with a couple of dogs and the odd visitor. If you email during European daytime/evening,

I'll fix it for you within an hour or two. If you're outside my time zone (for example North America, or Australia) it might take a little longer!

Now, go and get the recordings, and once you have them, we'll talk about the ideal set-up.

SECTION 1 - HYPNOSIS TRAINING AND CONDITIONING

5

WHY YOU NEED THIS TRAINING

IF YOU'RE TRYING hypnosis for the first time, you'll benefit from some training and conditioning before we set to work on your Motivation in Part Two.

If you're confident with hypnosis, and ready to get stuck in to the serious stuff, you can skip straight to Chapter 11 and start the main program.

However, even if you don't want to read this section, I'd still encourage you to play the two training recordings at least once, to refresh your skills and get you in the mood, so to speak.

You can complete the whole training program in an hour or so, and doing so will greatly enhance the effects of the main recordings in Part 2.

If you've never tried hypnosis before, please do this training program. The recordings in Part 2 are *Intermediate* level and are designed to work best with clients who are well-conditioned in advance. These *Beginner* scripts will get you ready.

This initial training program contains two fifteen-minute recordings:

1. **Training Session 1 - Basic Induction.** This first session will allow you to experience hypnosis and trance, maybe for the first time in your life. You can repeat it as often as you like, and the more you use it, the more comfortable and confident you'll become with the whole hypnosis process.

You don't have to do anything except relax and enjoy the experience.

2. **Training Session 2 - Visualisation and Calibration.** In the second script, you'll explore your own capabilities whilst in hypnosis. You'll discover your *modality*; how you see, hear, and feel whilst hypnotised.

Once again, you may repeat this session several times, and your depth of trance and imagination skills will improve each time.

By the time you've completed these two sessions, you'll be ready to move on and get serious about your Motivation.

6

SET-UP AND PREPARATION

IN ORDER TO give yourself the best opportunity for success with hypnosis, you need to pay attention to your immediate environment. The more ideal you can make the set-up, the more relaxed you will become, and the fewer distractions are likely to occur.

Most of these instructions are simple common sense, but you'd be surprised at how many people ignore the obvious!

Privacy

In the early stages, whilst you're learning the basics, you need to shut yourself away somewhere private, and make sure you won't be disturbed. There's nothing to be gained by having someone else listening in or involving themselves in the process.

If you live alone, it's simple. If you have family or flatmates, it's up to you if you decide to tell them what you are planning to do. In my view it's always better to come clean, because when you finally shut yourself away to practice, you really need to eliminate any concerns that you're doing something covert or sneaky, or that someone might think it's silly if they accidentally discover what you're doing.

You don't want to be trying to descend into trance whilst keeping one ear open for approaching footsteps!

If you're going to eliminate distraction - which is essential for this process to work - you must *control your environment.*

Tranquillity

Silence in your hypnosis environment is ideal, although it may be difficult to achieve, especially if you live in a city. Nevertheless you should strive to establish the quietest possible space for your hypnosis.

Close the doors and windows and switch your phone to 'Flight Mode' so that it won't ring or vibrate. Anything which disrupts your concentration whilst you're doing the exercise might take you back to the beginning. Once you're well-practiced at this, you'll be able to deal with external sounds as part of the trance, but at the beginning, until you've mastered the process, you need to eliminate as much external disturbance as possible.

You'll probably be using headphones, which will block most external noise, depending on the kind you use.

I regularly used headphones for my clients and a headset microphone for myself in my London practice, which was just 2000ft below the flight path for Heathrow airport!

Your Personal Comforts

As you've understood, achieving the hypnotic state will always go better if you eliminate distractions, which includes physical distractions.

- Wear clothing that doesn't pinch or constrict. You may want to remove your shoes, belt, and watch.
- Visit the the bathroom before you start. A call of nature half-way though your session is difficult to ignore, and it will probably mean starting the session all over again.
- Make sure the room temperature is comfortable; not too cool and not too warm.

Where to Sit

If you visit a professional hypnotherapist, you'll rarely see a couch or flat-bed in their office, and there's a good reason for this.

As you can imagine, taking people into a state of deep relaxation can run the risk of them falling asleep, especially if they arrive tired for the session. If you're lying down, the risk is increased, because this is most people's natural sleeping position.

If a client nods off during hypnosis, the session is essentially over, because your hearing shuts down as soon as you're asleep and nothing goes in, apart from the noise of a fire alarm or a wake-up call!

Falling asleep during hypnosis is not uncommon, and it's completely harmless. Once asleep, the hypnosis is muted, and anything that happens whilst you're asleep won't be effective.

Within the scope of the hypnosis exercises you'll do in this course, you can be sure that you'll eventually wake up 'out of trance', so no harm done. But you could waste time and effort, which is why you should try to avoid lying horizontally if possible.

Of course, if you have no alternative comfortable location, the hypnosis itself will work fine on a couch or bed, but you need to be aware of the heightened risk of snoozing through the best bit!

The ideal situation is a comfortable chair: even a recliner if you have access to one. Try to have your legs uncrossed and your feet flat on the floor. You should make sure your head and neck are supported with a cushion.

Where to put your hands is really related to how you would normally sit to relax. I've found that most clients like it if I give them cushion to put on their lap and then they can rest their hands on it.

A competent professional hypnotist can work on clients

in almost any position, and if you've ever seen a good stage hypnotist, you'll have seen subjects put into trance whilst standing up. This is genuine, but it takes special training and immense confidence to master.

For your purposes, you should try to get as close to the picture as you can manage. As long as you're comfortable, and you don't need to tense any muscles to maintain your position, this will work just fine.

Stimulants

Stimulants can be an issue, so you should avoid them. Coffee in particular can inhibit relaxation, so it's best to avoid drinking it before you're going to work on your hypnosis skills.

Later, once you've mastered dropping in and out of hypnosis at will, it won't make much difference. But in the early stages, you're trying to eliminate every possible obstacle to you being able to enjoy the relaxation state that leads to hypnotic trance.

If you're a smoker, especially if you're using hypnosis in order to help you quit, I recommend that you thoroughly cleanse your breath and hands before you start. In hypnosis, your senses can sometimes sharpen unexpectedly, and the smell of tobacco could become intrusive once all other distractions are suppressed or eliminated, which could trigger a craving.

Of course – and this probably goes without saying – alcohol and drugs don't go well with hypnosis. It's virtually impossible to hypnotise a drunk, and although I did once manage to put a hardcore stoner into a deep trance - after many attempts - the work we tried to do once he was hypnotised was completely ineffective!

Other drugs are mainly stimulants, and it's pointless to try.

Light and Dark

Given the choice I would always prefer to practice hypnosis in a dimmer room. You may have to open and close your eyes a number of times during the process, and if the room is bright this can tend to kick you out of trance more quickly.

How dark is really a matter of personal preference. During the day you should close your shades or blinds so that there is still natural light in the room, but no bright light source. If you're practicing in the evening, a side-lamp is better than a bright ceiling lamp. Try to make sure it's out of your line of sight.

That's just about it for your environment. Most of these

tips are obvious, but they all combine to create the most conducive situation for you to succeed at hypnosis, so try to consider each one in terms of its practicality for you.

So, you've got your recording ready, and you're seated and relaxed in a comfortable, private environment.

You're all set, so let's get on with the first exercise.

7

STAGE ONE, SIMPLE INDUCTION AND EMERGE

What You'll Be Doing

IN THIS FIRST EXERCISE, we're going to use a standard hypnosis *induction* to start to get you used to how hypnosis works.

If you've visited a professional hypnotherapist in the past, it's possible that the induction part of your session may have been quite a prolonged affair. Many therapists use a technique called 'progressive relaxation' to take you gradually into a light trance, and then slowly deepen the state over anything up to an hour. This works fine for most people, but it takes a long time.

Rapid Induction

A famous American hypnotherapist, Dave Elman, having observed the apparent need to repeat this long-winded conditioning exercise, developed a very successful alternative which accelerates the induction process. I have been using this *Elman Induction* with clients for more than a decade, and found that it works well every time.

This induction compresses the repetitive conditioning into a series of brief *mini-inductions* which start to induce hypnosis through relaxation, then momentarily wake up the subject, before repeating the process again and again. The technique ensures that each time the subject opens his or her eyes, then drops back towards the trance state, they go deeper.

The result is a nicely hypnotised subject in a matter of a few short minutes. This is the technique we will be using in our first Training Exercise.

What To Expect

You won't be expected to make any earth-shattering discoveries at first, however each time you repeat this exercise you'll find that you'll become more confident and inquisitive.

Whilst you're in this light hypnotic state, you may find that you can begin to visualise scenes, places, or events. Alternately you may experience feelings or emotions, which can often become quite intense.

How you experience hypnosis will depend on you as an individual, whether you're principally visual, auditory or kinaesthetic by nature, or maybe a combination of any or all of these.

After an appropriate period of quiet time, my voice will gently emerge you from your hypnotic state, until you're wide awake, back in the room, and feeling great.

During Your Trance

Hypnosis is completely safe, and you will never lose your ability to wake yourself up if you feel uncomfortable with what's going on. The likelihood is that you'll wonder about this, sometime during your experience, but you'll feel so good that you won't feel the need to try to wake yourself up. I invite you to test this for yourself once you've gone through the induction stage.

There are three accepted stages of hypnotic trance which most professional hypnotherapists use. For the purpose of this explanation, we'll call them *light, medium, and deep.* In professional practice, the *deep* state is often used for treating really serious psychological conditions, as well as medical and dental anaesthesia.

It's unlikely (though possible) that you'll ever reach a state of deep (*comatose*) hypnotic trance using recorded hypnosis. Even if you do, the techniques contained in these scripts will work in exactly the same way, to emerge you back to your full waking state when it's time.

In this first exercise, we'll be targeting the *light* state. In this state, most people remain fully aware of where they are and what's going on around them, but they choose to 'switch off' that consciousness and 'go inside' to explore their own internal thoughts, images, and feelings.

You may achieve this light state on your very first attempt. You may even recognise it when it happens, or you may perhaps feel that nothing has changed, and you're just relaxing in a chair with your eyes closed. It doesn't matter, because each time you go into hypnosis you'll go deeper than the last time, and you'll discover new sensations and experiences which will encourage you to go further.

Remember, it's a *conditioning* process, and the more often you do it, the better you'll become.

When you emerge from your first hypnotic experience,

we're going to conduct a little de-brief, so that you can reflect on how you got on.

So, make yourself comfortable, put on your headphones, and when you're ready, **start the recording.**

De-Brief

Welcome back!

How was that for you? Why don't you stretch now, I'm sure you feel like it. You completed the exercise really well.

Now, just take moment to reflect on what happened. You might remember everything, or you might remember nothing at all. It may have seemed like a really short time, or alternately you might feel like you've been gone for ages. I can tell you that the whole exercise took less than fifteen minutes.

When you're completely ready, you're going to start the recording again and repeat the experience, but this time you will easily go much deeper into hypnosis, and each time that you do this you will be able to go deeper still.

Right now, I suggest you get up and walk around for a few

minutes, maybe have a cup of tea or a glass of water. Remember, no coffee and preferably no smoking! Then when you're ready to try it again, come back and make yourself comfortable.

De-Briefing Yourself

After the first time you try the exercise, there may be things that you noticed which you can change in order to make it easier next time. Just run through the check-list below, and make any adjustments before the next repetition.

- *Temperature*: was I too warm or too cold?
- *Comfort*: how was my seating position, the position of my hands, and so on?
- *Volume*: was the recording too loud, too soft?
- *Brightness*: do I need to lighten or darken the room?
- *External sounds*: was I distracted? Do I need to stop anything, close any windows, and so on?

These are small things, but any one of them can detract from the overall experience, so it's really worth taking a little time to get everything right, so that there are no obstacles to you achieving that wonderful depth of relaxation which hypnosis offers.

You can go on repeating this exercise as many times as you like. You'll be the best judge how well it's working for you, and you'll notice the progressive conditioning as you try it again, and again.

Although my voice is guiding you, the actual hypnosis is coming from you. You're allowing it to happen, and it is happening. That's the essence of hypnosis.

You should not think about moving on until you're entirely comfortable with this first exercise. Many people report that the second time they do it, it's much more effective than the first, and this is the conditioning effect we discussed earlier. Just keep repeating the recording as many times as you like. There's no such thing as too much practice!

Next, in Stage Two, we're going to use the skills that you've developed in Stage One to train you to use the hypnotic state to do new things.

8

STAGE TWO: CALIBRATION - A DAY AT THE BEACH

Exercise Two

NOW WE'LL USE another recorded script which starts off with a similar induction to the one we used before.

Once you're in trance, you will be given a *trigger word*, which is 'BEACH' and your task is to experience everything associated with being at a beach.

The idea is to *calibrate* you so that you'll be able to tell if you're predominately *visual*, *auditory* or *kinaesthetic*, whether you see, hear, or feel more strongly in hypnosis. How you experience the beach will determine what we call your *modality*, and this will help you to anticipate and understand how to harness hypnosis' benefits in the future.

You'll be using your powerful imagination, which allows you to roam freely in hypnosis. If you're primarily visual, you may be able to generate a clear image of the beach scene and to be able to describe it, either during the trance or afterwards.

Maybe you'll be primarily auditory, in which case you may hear the sounds of the waves, or children playing in the sand.

Alternately - if you are primarily kinaesthetic - you might feel the breeze on your face, or smell the salty air.

It's entirely possible that you may experience more than one of these modalities, which is great, and it's also possible you'll form a multi-sensual impression, neither one thing or another, but which will work just as well.

This sessions called "Hypnosis Training Session 2" and you can download or stream it just the same as the first one.

Parts of the script may be familiar to you, which should help you to drop into hypnosis very easily. However, some of the parts are shortened because you simply don't need all the deepening techniques now that you've become proficient.

Again, if you insist on recording your own scripts, this one's printed long-hand in the next chapter.

Once you have the recording ready, make yourself comfortable and quickly run through the checklist below:

- Switch your phone to Flight Mode if you've downloaded the recording. If you're going to stream it (over wi-fi) select the setting which leaves the wi-fi on but turns calls and notifications off.
- Make sure you won't be disturbed for around fifteen minutes.
- Visit the bathroom if you need to.
- Take a few moments to acclimatise yourself to any sounds that you may hear during the exercise, and explain to yourself that these will not disturb you.

When you're completely ready, **start the recording** and enjoy the trance!

De-Brief

If you followed the preparation instructions and stuck to the recorded script, you should be quite amazed by now, at your own ability to enter hypnosis and what you can do whilst you're there.

The Beach scene often evokes powerful imagery or sensations in people who try this exercise, and I'm sure you experienced something like that too. If, for some reason, it wasn't as vivid or literal as you'd hoped, don't worry. Just play it again, even two or three times, and the effect will increase as you get more proficient at exercising your powerful imagination.

You'll remember from the introduction that this was called a *calibration* exercise, and the idea was to try to discover your modality, that is to say are you predominately visual, auditory or kinaesthetic. Your experience at the beach should have given you a good idea of this.

Did you see the colours? Were they bright or dull? Did you see movement, or was it like a post-card? If any of these statements are true for you, make a mental note of the answers so that you can build your future visualisations around your strengths.

Maybe you didn't see much, but you heard the sounds. Could you hear the waves, the seagulls, the people talking and kids playing? Maybe you heard a more elaborate sound-track, like a beach bar or a restaurant with music. Again, try to recall what you were hearing and make a mental note of how vivid it was, how complex and/or realistic the experience.

Or maybe you mainly felt *things*, like breeze, smell, or texture? Maybe what you experienced was an 'impression' of the beach, enough to convince you that you were there, even though you couldn't see or hear very much? That's called kinaesthetic.

You should now be able to assess and decide your dominant *modality*. If you can't do it yet, I suggest you run the recording again, now that you know what to expect, and spend some more time at the beach!

You'll have accomplished this part of the mission when you're able to say to yourself: *"I am predominately visual/auditory/kinaesthetic."*

Remember, you don't have to have only ONE modality, but you should try to identify your dominant one, because that's the way that you'll approach your exercises when you start doing more interesting things with your hypnosis.

By now you should be dropping easily into trance, and you should be totally confident in your own ability. You can completely let go and enjoy the experience, and you should also have convinced yourself that each time you do it, you go deeper.

Once you feel comfortable with this process, you'll be ready to move on to the main event.

See you there.

9

THE TRAINING TRANSCRIPTS

Session 1 Transcript

WHEN YOU'RE ready to enter hypnosis, take a long deep breath and hold it for a few seconds. As you exhale this breath, allow your eyes to close and let go of the surface tension in your body. Just let your body relax as much as possible right now.

Now, place your awareness on your eye muscles and relax the muscles around your eyes to the point they just won't work. When you're sure they're so relaxed that as long as you hold on to this relaxation they just won't work, hold on to that relaxation and test them to make sure THEY WON'T WORK.

Now, this relaxation you have in your eyes is the same quality of relaxation that I want you to have throughout your whole body. So, just let this quality of relaxation flow through your whole body from the top of your head to the tips of your toes.

Now, we can deepen this relaxation much more. In a moment, I'm going to have you open and close your eyes. When you close your eyes, that's your signal to let this feeling of relaxation become 10 times deeper. All you have to do is want it to happen and you can make it happen very easily. OK, now, open your eyes... now close your eyes and feel that relaxation flowing through your entire body, taking you much deeper. Use your wonderful imagination and imagine your whole body is covered and wrapped in a warm blanket of relaxation.

Now, we can deepen this relaxation much more. In a moment, I'm going to have you open and close your eyes one more time. Again, when you close your eyes, double the relaxation you now have. Make it become twice as deep. OK, now once more, open your eyes ... close your eyes and double your relaxation... Good. Let every muscle in your body become so relaxed that as long as you hold on to this quality of relaxation, every muscle of your body will not work.

In a moment, I'm going to have you open and close your eyes one more time. Again, when you close your eyes, double the relaxation you now have. Make it become twice as deep. OK, now once more open your eyes... close your eyes and double your relaxation... Good. Let every muscle in your body become so relaxed that as long as you hold on to this quality of relaxation every muscle of your body will not work.

Now, that's complete physical relaxation. I want you to know that there are two ways a person can relax. You can physically relax and you can relax mentally. You already proved that you can relax physically, now let me show you how to relax mentally.

In a moment, I'll ask you to begin slowly counting backwards, in your mind, from 100. Now, here's the secret to mental relaxation; with each number you say, you'll double your mental relaxation. With each number you say, let your mind become twice as relaxed. Now, if you do this, by the time you reach the number 97, or maybe even sooner, your mind will have become so relaxed, you will actually have relaxed all the rest of the numbers (that would have come after 97) right out of your mind. There just won't be any more numbers. Those numbers will leave, if you will them away. Now, start with the idea that you will make that happen and you can easily dispel them from your mind.

Now, in your mind say the first number, 100 and double your mental relaxation. Now the next number..... Good.... Now double that mental relaxation. Let those numbers already start to fade. Next number.....Double your mental relaxation. Start to make those numbers leave. They'll go if you will them away. Now, they'll be gone. Dispel them. Banish them. Make it happen, you can do it, Push them out. Make it happen! THEY ARE ALL GONE

That's fine. The mind is relaxed and the body's relaxed. Just let yourself relax much more with every single breath. And I do want your body to relax just a little bit more so let me help you do that. This time I will count from 5 down to 1. With every number I say, let your mind and body relax together like a team so that by the time I reach the count of one, mentally and physically you easily let yourself relax much more. All right?

5-deeper--that's good—4 - 3 --that's fine-2 – deeper down and - --------------- 1.

That's great, doing fine. I'd like you now to see if you would allow yourself, to let yourself, to go to your very basement of your ability to relax. And you know there is no real basement of a person's ability because we've never found a basement, only on every particular instant in time your basement can be many, many times deeper. And I'll help you to get there.

I want you to imagine that there are three more levels to take you to your basement of your relaxation.--levels -A, B, and C. To get to-level A,- you--simply- double the relaxation that you have now. To get to level B, you must double the relaxation you have in level A. And finally to get to your basement, you must at least double what you have in level B. To help you with this, I want you to use that powerful imagination of yours. And I want you to imagine that you're standing at the top of your own private escalator, like they have at the shopping centre only this is your own private escalator.

I am going to count to 3 - and at the count of 3, you'll step onto your escalator that will be taking you from where you are now down to level A, double the relaxation that you have now. When you get there, you'll let yourself know by simply raising one finger gently. Here we go-1-2-3. Step on to the escalator and go down, deeper down, doubling that relaxation which feels so good. When you reach the next level, step off your escalator and relax. Good, wonderful.

Now in a moment we're going to go from level A to level B. To get to level B, you simply have to double the relaxation that you're allowing in level A. Just let it grow twice as deep. All right. Imagine yourself at the top of your next escalator. Here we go, 1-2-3 and step on... Let it take you all the way down where you will have doubled your relaxation. Now, if you're following these instructions, you may find it difficult to move your finger, but that doesn't matter at all. But try anyway. Just take all the time you need to get to level B--- and when you arrive at the bottom of that escalator, step off and relax. Good.

Now there's one more level that I'd like you to go to: Level C -- the very basement of your ability to relax. Once more, find yourself at the top of that escalator. At the count of three, step on and it will take you all the way down to level C -- the very basement of your ability to relax today. Here we go: -1-2-3. - deeper-deeper-letting go-deeper-deeper-deeper-to the very basement of your relaxation-drifting down-much more relaxed. OK. That's fine. Way down. Now just let yourself stay there for a moment and notice at this level every breath you exhale just easily helps you relax even more. Every breath takes you deeper and deeper relaxed.

Now as you relax, drifting deeper with every word I speak, the first thing I would like you to know is how much I appreciate and admire you for the decision you have made to try hypnosis for yourself and to explore the wonderful benefits that it can add to your life.

Now you have those physical signs that allow you to know that you have moved from one conscious state to another in a calm and confident way. In this calm and confident state you can offer yourself generous portions of self confidence... large helpings of self-esteem, breathing out self-doubt as you relax even deeper and continue to enjoy the journey towards your goal.

Now you're going to take a short period of silence, relaxed in this beautiful hypnotic state, and experience whatever comes to you. See what you see, hear what you hear, feel what you feel, and simply let the waves of physical and mental relaxation wash over you.

(Pause)

You've done great.

In a moment, I'm going to count from ONE up to THREE. At the count of three your eyes are going to open, become fully alert, totally refreshed. Any cobwebs that you might have had, any sleepiness of mind is going to dissolve and disappear, and you're going to feel bright eyed and full of energy. You'll be fully alert and wonderful and marvellous in every way.

ONE, slowly easily and gently feel yourself coming back up to your full awareness.

At the count of TWO you're still relaxed and calm but notice that your eyes under your eyelids feel as if they're clearing, kind of like they're being bathed in a sparkling cool mountain stream, you feel GREAT.

On the next count those eyes are going to open, totally alert, fully refreshed, just feeling excited, wonderful, in every way, and every time you go into hypnosis you can let yourself go deeper than the time before because you know that just feels good.

All right, get ready, and on the count of THREE open those eyes and notice how good you feel.

Session 2

Self-Calibration Transcript

When you are ready to enter trance once more, take a long deep breath and hold it for a few seconds. Now exhale this breath and allow your eyes to close and let go of the surface tension in your body. Just let your body relax as much as possible as you've done so many times before.

Now, place your awareness on your eye muscles and relax the muscles around your eyes to the point they just won't work. When you're sure they're so relaxed that as long as you hold on to this relaxation they just won't work, hold on to that relaxation and test them to make sure THEY JUST WON'T WORK.

Now, this relaxation you have in your eyes is the same quality of relaxation that I want you to have throughout your whole body. So, just let this quality of relaxation flow through your whole body from the top of your head to the tips of your toes.

Now, you know that can deepen this relaxation much more. In a moment, you're going to open and close your eyes. When you close your eyes, that's your signal to let this feeling of relaxation become 10 times deeper. You want it to happen and you have proved that you can make it happen very easily. OK, now, open your eyes... and close your eyes and feel that relaxation flowing through your entire body, taking you much deeper. Use your wonderful imagination and imagine your whole body is covered and wrapped in a warm blanket of relaxation.

Now, you can deepen this relaxation much more. In a moment, you're going to open and close your eyes one more time. Again, when you close your eyes, double the relaxation you now have. Make it become twice as deep. OK, now once more, open your eyes ... and close your eyes and double your relaxation. That feels SO good. Let every muscle in your body become so relaxed that as long as you hold on to this quality of relaxation, every muscle of your body will not work.

In a moment, you're going to open and close your eyes one more time. Again, when you close your eyes, double the relaxation you have now. Make it become twice as deep, as you did so many times before. OK, now once more open your eyes... and close your eyes and double your relaxation... excellent. Let every muscle in your body become so relaxed that as long as you hold on to this quality of relaxation every muscle in your body just will not work.

Now that you're totally physically relaxed. You are going to easily relax mentally. You already proved that you can relax physically, now you know exactly how to relax mentally.

In a moment, you'll to begin slowly counting backwards, in your mind, from 100. And with each number you say, you will double your mental relaxation. With each number that you say, let your mind become twice as relaxed. Start to count, and by the time you reach the number 97, or maybe even sooner, your mind will have become so relaxed, you will actually have relaxed all the rest of the numbers right out of your mind. There just won't be any more numbers. Those numbers will leave, if you make them go away. You have proved that you can make that happen and you can easily dispel them from your mind. Now, start counting backwards from 100 and make those numbers disappear. Each number that you say will double your mental relaxation. Start to make those numbers leave. They'll go if you will them away. Now, they'll be gone. Dispel them. Banish them. Make it happen, you can do it, Push them out. Make it happen! Good, THEY ARE ALL GONE

Well done. Your mind is relaxed and your body's relaxed. Just let yourself relax much more with every single breath. And I do want your body to relax just a little bit more so let me help you do that. This time I will count from 5 down to 1. With every number I say, let your mind and body relax together like a team so that by the time I reach the count of one, mentally and physically you easily let yourself relax much more. All right?

5-deeper--that's good—4 - 3 --that's fine-2 – deeper down and -
-------------- 1.

That's great, doing fine. Now that you are so relaxed, you're going to go even deeper, and you already know how to do this. Imagine the escalators which will carry you down towards the basement of your ability to relax even deeper.

You know that there are three more levels to take you to your basement of your relaxation.--levels -A, B, and C. As you go deeper to each level double the relaxation that you have now. Use that powerful imagination of yours so that you're standing at the top of your private escalator and when I count to 3, Step on to your escalator and it will be taking you from where you are now down to level A, double the relaxation that you have now. When you get there, you'll signal by simply raising one finger gently. Here we go-1-2-3 and down you go, deeper into relaxation. Good, wonderful. (Pause)

Now in a moment we're going to go from level A to level B just like before. To get to level B, you simply have to double the relaxation that you're allowing in level A. Just let it grow twice as deep. All right. Imagine yourself at the top of your next escalator. Here we go, 1-2-3. And step on. Let it take you all the way down where you will have doubled your relaxation. Just take all the time you need to get to level B--- [WAIT]--Good.

Now there's one more level that you know you can go to: level C--the very basement of your ability to relax. Once more, find yourself at the top of that escalator. At the count of three, , it'll take you all the way down to level C -- the very basement of your ability to relax. Here we go-1-2-3. Step on... -deeper-deeper-letting go-deeper-deeper-deeper-to the very basement of your relaxation-drifting down-much more relaxed. OK. That's fine. Way down.

Now just let yourself stay there for a moment and notice at this level every breath you exhale just easily helps you relax even more. Every breath takes you deeper and deeper relaxed.

And now you know how amazing and easy it is to get to this deep place of relaxation, and you are welcome to remain in this beautiful place as long as you want and to come here again any time that you like, because you KNOW how to relax your body and mind completely and let go so you relax so completely.

Now you have those physical signs that allow you to know that you have moved from one conscious state to another in a calm and confident way. In this calm and confident state you can offer yourself generous portions of self confidence... large helpings of self-esteem, breathing out self-doubt as you relax even deeper and continue to enjoy the journey towards your goal.

Take a few moments to appreciate the peace and tranquillity in this deep place that you have brought yourself to. (Short Pause)

Now, imagine you are at the Beach and it's a lovely day.

(Pause) See what you see, hear what you hear, feel what you feel. Take a moment to experience how it is, there at the beach. Allow your powerful, wonderful imagination to transport you there and be at the beach, however that is for you.

If you can see where you are, say "I can see it", or if you can hear the sounds around you say "I can hear it" and if you can feel the warmth, the breeze, and the texture of the sand, say "I can feel it". Go on, just say out loud what is happening to you, and your imagination of this wonderful beach will grow stronger. Allow yourself to feel how good it is to be at the beach, how relaxed and comfortable you are and just rest there for a few moments, taking it all in.

(Pause)

And now you know new things, and that knowledge empowers you. You know about this beach, and how wonderfully relaxing it is to be here, and you know that you can return here any time you choose because you have proven the power of your wonderful imagination and your amazing ability to bring yourself to this wonderful state of deep relaxation any time that you choose, so easily. And I want you now to remember what happened to you at the beach today, what you saw and what you heard and what you felt, so that you can remind yourself later about this amazing beach and your clever ability to come here again. Just relax quietly for a few moments and take it all in.

(Silence for two minutes)

Now it's time for you to leave the beach for now, so let your imagination gently fade.

You've done great. PAUSE. In a moment I'm going to count from ONE up to THREE. At the count of three your eyes are going to open, become fully alert, totally refreshed. Any cobwebs that you might have had, any sleepiness of mind is going to dissolve and disappear, and you're going to feel bright eyed and full of energy.

You'll be fully alert and wonderful and marvellous in every way. ONE, slowly easily and gently feel yourself coming back up to your full awareness.

At the count of TWO you're still relaxed and calm but notice that your eyes under your eyelids feel as if they're clearing, kind of like they're being bathed in a sparkling cool mountain stream, you feel GREAT.

On the next count those eyes are going to open, totally alert, fully refreshed, just feeling excited, wonderful, in every way, and every time you go into hypnosis you can let yourself go deeper than the time before because you know that just feels good. All right, get ready, and on the count of THREE open those eyes and notice how good you feel.

10

A BRIEF HISTORY OF HYPNOSIS

IF YOU'RE interested in how hypnosis and hypnotherapy evolved to where we are today, this short section might interest you.

If you'd rather get stuck in to the real stuff, you can skip this section; it won't make any difference to your experience with hypnosis.

What most people understand about hypnosis is largely grounded in two areas. On a personal level, you may have tried it, or know someone else who has tried it. Alternately, you'll have seen it on TV or at a theatre show.

The fundamental technique of hypnosis is 'congruent communication', particularly verbal communication. But the myriad of studies suggests that the process is much more complicated and sophisticated than that.

The urban legend that we only use 10% or 20% of our brains is an oversimplification, but it's entirely possible that we are only 20% competent in the use of *all* our brain faculties. This, of course, is the essence of training of any kind.

Hypnosis is a major part of the armoury of Witch Doctors and Shaman, as well as Faith Healers and Con Artists, who've been around since the dawn of time. It could be argued that the radicalisation of vulnerable young people by fundamentalist zealots owes a lot to hypnosis.

Some schools of thought believe that part of natural evolution is the understanding of the conscious ability to tap into the subconscious rhythmic operation of the brain and the body as a whole.

It seems likely that all the faculties required to enter a hypnotic state exist within a person's own mind, and that the role of the outside force such as the shaman or hypnotist is to guide the subject into accessing resources which are normally hidden, and to implant the skills to enable them to do it repetitively.

In the 18th century, a physician called Franz Mesmer identified the hypnotic state, and coined the term "animal magnetism", believing that it was an intangible fluid blessed with healing powers that was able to exert mutual influence between the Universe, the Earth and Animal Bodies, especially humans. He equated this fluid state as being magnetic in nature, and conducted many experiments using magnetism to demonstrate a natural or enhanced behaviour in humans and animals. In his most famous case, Mesmer treated a blind pianist and apparently restored her sight.

Unfortunately, given the political and religious environment of the day, Mesmer was labelled a fraud, and died in relative obscurity in Switzerland in 1815. However he left behind the term *mesmerised*.

Two notable British pioneers of hypnosis took the science forward in the 1800's. James Esdaile was a surgeon who used hypnotic anaesthesia successfully in hundreds of surgical operations, and in modern hypnosis the deepest state of trance is often still referred to as the *Esdaile State*.

James Braid, also a physician, was particularly struck by an exhibition of mesmerism by the French expert Lafontaine, and took up intensive research thereafter. During this time there was some confusion as to whether hypnosis was a state of sleep, and Braid's induction methods were based on eye fatigue. Braid's research has only become relevant and interesting in the 20th and 21st centuries, and he did not achieve much of a profile in his day.

After Braid, recorded research moved to France, and great strides were made in the use of hypnosis as a receptacle for suggestion techniques, and the language structures of *suggestion* started to develop. Sigmund Freud experimented with hypnosis for some time but eventually discarded it, probably because it did not offer him many advantages in his psychoanalytical work.

Fast-forward to the 1950s, and the era of Dave Elman. Elman was relatively low-key, but was widely regarded and respected in the medical and psychological communities in the USA. Elman may be credited with having taken away a lot of the mystique surrounding hypnosis.

Hypnotists of the day appear to have been somewhat anal in enhancing and dramatising the science and the therapies involved in it. There was also a great deal of fear around at the time, and the spectre of *electric shock therapy* in the mental health system frightened many people away from what they saw as *mental medicine.*

Elman dramatically simplified the definitions of hypnosis and also the techniques used to induce it. These days, confident hypnotists still employ the Elman induction, because it enables them to take most patients into a appropriate state of trance in between five and ten minutes, rather than the thirty minute inductions favoured by the more traditional branch of science.

I use the Elman induction (a lot) in my own hypnotherapy sessions, and it works well on almost everyone, saving a lot of time in the preamble stage and enabling more of the session to be devoted to actually solving the clients' issues.

Post flower-power, a new branch of hypnosis and psychoanalysis emerged, most notably under the leadership of Richard Bandler and John Grinder. The original concepts of *Neuro Linguistic Programming (NLP)* were laid out for the world in their breakthrough book "Frogs to Kings". Richard Bandler has gone on to have a colourful career but remains at the pinnacle of the NLP movement. His description of NLP as *waking hypnosis* may be viewed as something of a paradox, since modern science confirms that all hypnosis is conducted in a waking state.

Nevertheless, NLP aids the comprehension of language; how spoken conversation can be formatted to cut through someone's critical function and exert positive influence on the subconscious and instinctive part of the personality.

If you want to see a consummate NLP practitioner in action, I recommend watching one of Bill Clinton's big speeches, which can be found on YouTube. If you watch it, try to identify the small snippets of patterned language which may sound occasionally incongruous, but are carefully crafted to induce approval, compliance, or a favourable opinion from the audience.

Probably the best-known hypnotist in the UK, and subsequently in America, is Paul McKenna. McKenna makes hypnosis look easy, but he is without doubt an outstanding exponent of the science. McKenna is not just able to hypnotise people, but he has the sixth sense which allows him to quickly empathise with the subject, and thinking on his feet, use rapid techniques to effect a change. He's rich because he's good at this. I've spent some time training with both Richard Bandler and Paul McKenna, separately and together, and the experience was scintillating.

Many people credit Dave Elman with the quotation *"all hypnosis is self hypnosis."* The role of the hypnotist can be as a trainer. If you ever learned to ski, you can understand how it's possible to train a new skill into someone of any age from a zero start, usually in a matter of hours.

Hypnosis is a similar process: you have all the resources to enable you to do this, but you need a guide and a trainer to explain the system by which you access them and make them work.

SECTION 2 - THE MOTIVATION CODE

11

THE MOTIVATION CODE

WELCOME (AGAIN) TO THE PROGRAM.

The three sessions in this series are progressive, so you should try to do them in order, at least the first time..

These scripts have been created and designed to work at an *intermediate* level, that is that you should be familiar with hypnosis, and have successfully gone into trance, before.

If you're new to hypnosis, or if it's been more than a few months since you last tried it, I recommend you first use my two training recordings, which were included in your download package. These will take you less than an hour to complete, and they'll condition you for the deeper level of hypnosis we're now going to be using.

Throughout the whole course, you'll be learning and absorbing new habits.

These aren't magic; they're the habits of successful high-achievers the world over. Once you start to employ these tools and systems, you'll be modelling the behaviour of the people you most want to emulate; those people that make life seem effortless, and always have lots of time to do things for themselves, because they've learned the most effective and efficient way of managing themselves through their daily challenges.

They've cracked the Motivation Code.

Here's what you can expect in the sessions;

Session One focuses on your desires, goals, and objectives, and teaches you define *destinations* and *journeys*. You'll sharpen your long-range focus so that you can start to gain perspective, and control your short-term challenges with micro-planning rituals. Once you rediscover the pleasures of successful outcomes, you'll channel your energy into getting past the hard stuff quickly, without prevarication.

Session Two borrows from the mindsets and rituals of Olympic athletes, to equip you with powerful secret weapons for getting off the start line, executing race strategy, and finishing strongly every time. Distractions fall away when you have just one important job to do!

Session Three reveals choices you hadn't considered, and shows you how to dump your complicated cocktail of negative thinking - *the bad code* - in a vault so secure that it simply won't come back to influence you in the future. Once you're free of your artificial emotional restraints, you'll see the full picture - maybe for the first time - and the immense potential you possess.

Once you have a clear target and a solid plan, and you replace that bad code you don't need any more, you won't recognise the old you any more.

You'll feel powerful, you'll radiate positive energy, and you'll join the legion of successful, motivated people who know how to use The Motivation Code to get what they want.

And you'll feel a whole lot better than you do right now!

WHEN YOU'RE ready to start, make yourself comfortable and make sure you won't be disturbed. Draw the shades, eliminate any distracting noises, and prepare yourself to be hypnotised. Each of the three recordings has a short introduction, or pre-amble, following which you'll begin the hypnosis.

Let's begin.

12

GETTING THE RECORDINGS

Getting Your Recordings

IF YOU ALREADY HAVE THE recordings, you can jump straight to **Session 1.**

If you came straight here and missed out Section One (Training and Conditioning), here's a reminder of how to access and use the recorded hypnosis sessions for this program.

I've simplified the access process so you should have no issues, but please get in touch if you do.

Let's get you organised right now:

When you click on this link (or type it into your browser

if you're reading the print version) it will open up a little form on your screen. Please enter your first name and your email address (so I know where to send your recordings) and submit the form.

That's all you need to do.

http://tiny.cc/amzmotv

Within a minute or two, you'll receive an email from **rick@ricksmithhypnosis.com**, containing your access information. Please keep this email safe, so you can access the sessions anytime.

It's not unknown for this first e-mail to go into your junk folder, so please check there first if you don't receive it within three minutes of registering.

The email you receive will direct you to the secure download page for this program. Once there, you'll have two options. You can use either or both:

On Your Phone or Tablet

Each session in the program has a Download button. When you click the button, the track will start to play. Simple!

On Your Computer

You can play the tracks on your computer in exactly the same way, however you can also download them to keep or share.

To do this, start the track using the Download button, then pause it and right click in the play-bar controls and choose Download.

The individual audio files are MP3's, the same as a song you might download from iTunes or Google Play.

Download the Whole Program

Because the tracks are longer (30-45 minutes each), and there are several tracks in each program, they've been compressed and packaged into what's called a 'Zip' file, to make them easier and faster to deliver by download.

If you opt to download the .zip file, you will get the complete program (it may take a few minutes) on your computer's hard drive. From there, you click on it and it will open and unpack the individual recordings as MP3's.

Once you can see each of the individual tracks, you can simply play each one by clicking on it, or you can transfer the tracks (just like music) to your phone or tablet, using whatever method you would usually use for songs. If you're struggling with this, ask a nearby teenager to help you!

Once you've done that, you can open your music player (such as iTunes) and find the track in the alphabetic list of all your stored music tracks. The artist name is Rick Smith.

If you download it to your 'Downloads' or 'Desktop', you can play the recordings direct, or open iTunes or your preferred music player, and import the file.

You can play it from there, or alternately you might decide to create a new Playlist (perhaps call it 'Hypnosis Sessions') and drag the track into it. Then you'll easily be able to find it, and when you sync to your phone or tablet next time, make sure you add the playlist and you'll be able to find it easily on your device, which is where you really need it to be.

On Your Phone or Tablet

Downloading the whole program's *zip* file to your phone or tablet isn't an option for most people, because these devices don't usually have a file system to open and store the tracks.

So instead, you can access the individual sessions and

play (stream) them live, wherever you have Wi-Fi or data available, from the Download Page (see above).

Your *welcome and access email* will show you where to find the recordings, and it's one simple click to start, pause, or stop them at any time.

If you decide to go this way, you can be up and running on your portable device within three minutes of clicking or typing the link below, and you can always go back and download the whole program when you're near your computer.

This means you can access the recordings from anywhere you have data access. Each recorded session is typically 30-40MB (equivalent to 6 - 8 mp3 songs), so please be careful if you have a limited data plan with your phone carrier. Wi-fi, particularly at home, is often free or unlimited, so that's the best and most economical way to access the recordings.

Whenever you use your portable device for playing sessions - which you'll be doing a lot throughout this program - please use headphones or earbuds for privacy. This also helps to block out external noises, which can be a distraction during your hypnosis sessions.

All set? Good. Here's the link that will get you rapid access to the recordings for this program.

http://tiny.cc/amzmotv

And if you hit any snags, email me here:

helpdesk@ricksmithhypnosis.com

13

SESSION 1 - WHAT'S YOUR DESTINATION

THIS INTRODUCTION IS ALSO INCLUDED *in the audio download for Session 1.*

Introduction to Session 1

Once you're seated comfortably and ready to begin, you'll first hear a short introduction or preamble about the work we're going to do in this session. I recommend you relax and close your eyes while this is playing, so you'll be ready to descend quickly into trance, once it's time.

In this first session, we'll be focusing on your attitude to structure and system; how you approach tasks each day and how you prioritise so that you're at your most effective, whilst acknowledging that some tasks are more challenging or unpleasant than others.

We'll also be exploring your goals and objectives, both in your day to day, and your life in general. Knowing what you want is very important, because it's easier to push yourself towards it when you're clear about what's at the end of your present journey.

I'll help you to begin to separate things from feelings, so you can learn to suppress displaced emotions which obstruct your progress and sap your energy and motivation.

We'll be going gently into hypnosis this time, to get the depth we need, and afterwards we'll review your experience before we move on to the next stage.

Now, if you're ready, and I know you are, please make sure you're comfortable, and start to relax.

PLAY THE SESSION 1 RECORDING NOW

Debrief

Welcome back! How as that for you? Let's just take moment to reflect on what happened. You might remember everything, or you might remember nothing at all. It may have seemed like a really short time, or alternately you might feel like you've been gone for ages. I can tell you that the whole exercise took around thirty minutes.

The objective of this session was to introduce you to the most basic and crucial aspects of motivating yourself, and those are system, structure and goal. You learned about the habits of successful motivated people, all of whom will use a task list in one form or another, usually preparing each days' task list the night before, making sure that every task is oriented towards their goal, or goals, whatever they may be.

It's a discipline which can sounds onerous at first, but now, you have a subconscious desire to try it and see how it works best for you. It really won't take very long, and as you will be establishing it as a daily habit, it will soon become automatic.

Please think about how you operate best, and choose the simplest and least time-consuming method you can.

Set a goal for the day, the week or the month, something achievable and which will satisfy you, then plot your course, plan each step, and keep focused on the end-state, because when you get there, you can rest.

It doesn't matter how you do it, but please do it, starting right away. You'll quickly establish a habit and a new focus, and it's the first building block in the structure of how this course will help you.

See you on the next session.

14

SESSION 2 - YOUR LINE OF COMMITMENT

THIS INTRODUCTION IS ALSO INCLUDED in the audio download for Session 2.

Session 2 Introduction

Welcome back.

In this session, you'll be going more quickly into trance, and we'll be exploring the practicalities of how you motivate yourself to act when you need to.

This script includes techniques that have been developed in the sports psychology field, where action and performance are the key elements of success. Pro athletes often have to put their bodies on the line, so commitment and motivation is central to their mindset.

You can take on these same skills and techniques, and make them work in your own situation.

So sit back, and let's explore that now.

PLAY THE SESSION 2 RECORDING NOW

Debrief

Welcome back! Time to stretch.

As you've learned in the past, everyone's experience of hypnosis is different. You may have gone very deep, and you may only remember bits of what just happened, or nothing at all.

Your subconscious mind has absorbed the key information about focusing on the objective you want, and using your line of commitment to kick-start your progress before it.

You don't need to be in hypnosis to use our line of commitment. It's there in front of you, all the time, even if you can't see it or visualise it, and all it takes is for you to gather your energy and resources and step over that line, and you're on your way to where you want to be.

Repeat this recording, and the others in the series, whenever you want to reinforce your new habits. The more often you practice, the more natural and automatic your upgraded behaviour will become.

Remember, doing something is ALWAYS preferable to doing nothing, in the long run.

See you in the next session.

15

SESSION 3 - HARD TALK

THIS INTRODUCTION IS ALSO INCLUDED in the audio download for Session 3.

Session 3 Introduction

Welcome back.

If you can imagine that every decision or action you take in life is decided by the winner of an ongoing contest between your logical brain and your emotional brain, you might conclude that your lack of motivation is primarily happening in your emotions.

When your logical brain is dominant, you power ahead with things, because at that moment, it makes perfect sense to you. You know what needs to happen, and the quicker you make it happen, the quicker your challenges are overcome, your problems solved, and the finish line behind you.

And that means you can then relax your logical brain, during your down time, and allow your emotional brain, the one that just wants you to enjoy yourself and feel good, to run riot.

However, not everyone's emotional brain is delivering happy stuff all the time. If things get out of whack, such as in cases of depression, and to a milder extent, lack of motivation, submitting to your emotional brain can be uncomfortable and unpleasant.

If you are clinically depressed, or suspect you are, you should be working with your physician, a talking therapist, or even a real-live hypnotherapist.

In this session we're going to be looking into the binary choices that your logical and emotional sides inflict on you. You'll learn to recognise which part's helping you and which is hindering you, and discover the power you have to switch from one to the other, as appropriate for your situation.

So let's get to work on that now.

· · ·

PLAY THE SESSION 3 RECORDING NOW

Debrief

Welcome back, I hope you enjoyed that?

Take a moment to stretch, that's right.

The key takeaway from this session is that you have all the personal power and resources to ensure your logical, sensible, motivated brain always remains dominant over your emotional, deceptive, troublesome brain.

You already knew this, but now you have shape and scale. It's a simple binary choice, and one which will become automatic for you the more time you exercise your control.

16

THE TRANSCRIPTS

Session 1 Transcript

Now, take a long deep breath and hold it for a few seconds. As you exhale this breath, allow your eyes to close and let go of the surface tension in your body. Just let your body relax as much as possible right now, as you've done before. We will take it slowly so you can go deeper than the last time.

Now, place your awareness on your eye muscles and relax the muscles around your eyes to the point they just won't work. When you're sure they're so relaxed that as long as you hold on to this relaxation they just won't work, hold on to that relaxation and test them to make sure THEY JUST WON'T WORK.

Now, this relaxation you have in your eyes is the same quality of relaxation that I want you to have throughout your whole body. So, just let this quality of relaxation flow through your whole body from the top of your head to the tips of your toes. Now, we can deepen this relaxation much more. In a moment, I'm going to have you open and close your eyes. When you close your eyes, that's your signal to let this feeling of relaxation become 10 times deeper. All you have to do is want it to happen and you can make it happen very easily.

Ok, now, open your eyes... now close your eyes and feel that relaxation flowing through your entire body, taking you much deeper. Use your wonderful imagination and imagine your whole body is covered and wrapped in a warm blanket of relaxation.

Now, we can deepen this relaxation much more. In a moment, I'm going to have you open and close your eyes one more time. Again, when you close your eyes, double the relaxation you now have. Make it become twice as deep.

Ok, now once more, open your eyes ... close your eyes and double your relaxation.. . good. Let every muscle in your body become so relaxed that as long as you hold on to this quality of relaxation, every muscle of your body will not work.

In a moment, I'm going to have you open and close your eyes one more time. Again, when you close your eyes, double the relaxation you now have. Make it become twice as deep. Ok, now once more open your eyes... close your eyes and double your relaxation... good. Let every muscle in your body become so relaxed that as long as you hold on to this quality of relaxation every muscle of your body will not work.

Now, that's complete physical relaxation. And you already know that there are two ways a person can relax. You can physically relax and you can relax mentally. You already proved that you can relax physically, now let me remind you how to relax mentally.

In a moment, I'll ask you to begin slowly counting backwards, out loud, from 100. Now, you know the secret to mental relaxation; with each number you say, double your mental relaxation. With each number you say, let your mind become twice as relaxed. Now, if you do this, by the time you reach the number 98, or maybe even sooner, your mind will have become so relaxed, you will actually have relaxed all the rest of the numbers that would have come after 98 right out of your mind. There just won't be any more numbers.

Now, you have to do this, I can't do it for you. Those numbers will leave if you will them away. Now start with the idea that you will make that happen and you can easily dispel them from your mind. Now, say the first number, 100 and double your mental relaxation: Now double that mental relaxation. Let those numbers already start to fade. 99

Double your mental relaxation. Start to make those numbers leave. They'll go if you will them away. 98: Now, they'll be gone. Dispel them. Banish them. Make it happen, you can do it, Push them out. Make it happen!

ARE THEY ALL GONE?

*That's fine. The mind is relaxed and the body's relaxed. Just let yourself relax much more with every general breath. And I do want your **body** to relax just a little bit more so let me help you do that. This time I will count from 10 down to 1. With every number I say, let your mind and body relax together like a team so that by the time I reach the count of one, mentally and physically you easily let yourself relax much more. All right?*

10- deeper - that's good -9-8-7-6 - that's fine -5-4-3 2-------------- -- 1.

That's good, doing fine. I'd like you now to see if you would allow yourself, to let yourself, to go to your very basement of your ability to relax. And you already know there is no real basement of a person's ability because we've never found a basement, only on every particular instant in time your basement can be many, many times deeper. And I'll help you to get there.

I want you to imagine that there are three more levels to take you to your basement of your relaxation.--levels -A, B, and C. To get to-level A,- you--simply- double the relaxation that you have now. To get to level B, you must double the relaxation you have in level A. And finally to get to Level C - your base-

ment of relaxation - you must at least double what you have in level B.

To help you with this, I want you to use that powerful imagination of yours. And I want you to imagine that you're standing at the top of your own private escalator, like they have at the shopping centre, only this is your own private escalator.

In a moment, I'm going to count to 3. At the count of 3, you'll step on to your escalator, which will be taking you from where you are now down to level A, double the relaxation that you have now. When you get there, you'll let yourself know by lifting a finger slightly, if you can.

Here we go-1-2-3. Step on to your escalator and feel yourself descending deeper, deeper down, becoming more relaxed the deeper you go. An as you imagine yourself arriving at the bottom of that escalator, ant Level A, allow yourself to step of and rest for a moment. Twice as relaxed.

Good, wonderful.

Now in a moment we're going to go from level A to level B. To get to level B, you simply have to double the relaxation that you're allowing in level A. Just let it grow twice as deep.

All right. Imagine yourself at the top of your escalator, and prepare to step on at the count of three.

Here we go, 1-2-3 and step on to that escalator. Let it take you all the way down where you will have doubled your relaxation. Just take all the time you need to get to level B, deeper down, doubling your relaxation. -Good. And when you arrive at Level B, just step lightly off and rest once more.

Now, if you're following these instructions, you may find it difficult to lift a finger, but try anyway.

Now there's one more level that I'd like you to go to: level C-- the very basement of your ability to relax. Once more, find yourself at the top of that escalator. At the count of three, you'll step on and it'll take you all the way down to level C -- the very basement of your ability to relax today. Here we go-1-2-3. Step on. Let yourself go down deeper-deeper-deeper-letting go-deeper-deeper-deeper-to your very basement of your relaxation-drifting down-much more relaxed. OK. That's fine. You're arriving at Level C now, so just step off.

Now just let yourself stay there for a moment and notice at this level every breath you exhale just easily helps you relax even more. Every breath takes you deeper and deeper relaxed.

The Work

Now that you're in this deeply tranquil, lazy state of being, you can take a moment to reflect on your positive attitude in looking for a better way to manage yourself and your approach to your challenges, responsibilities, and tasks. And you might be wondering if you're alone in seeking this knowledge, but of course you're not.

It's only natural for part of you to avoid or delay tricky or challenging tasks, and pretty much every human being is born with the same habits. We all know that resting is more enjoyable than working, so it will come as no surprise to you that people will naturally choose to rest if they can.

In the old days, our parent's generation might have described these habits as laziness, and sometimes they'd be right. But we know so much more now, because science has studied every aspect and combination of human behavior. It's now clear for everyone to see that there are many more complex emotions and interactions happening in your mind whenever you have to make choices about whether to so something or try to avoid it.

And you may have found in the past, when you were younger, that the presence of someone like a teacher, or a manager, or a parent, that you found it easier to complete your allotted tasks each day because you had the guiding hand of someone moving you along. Perhaps you had no need to question anything because you trusted whoever was guiding you, that they had your best interests in mind, and you simply progressed through your daily responsibilities as a matter of procedure.

Your emotions, how you felt about each task you were required to perform, weren't important, because your deal with your senior guide was that you would complete your tasks and then you could rest. A simple exchange of effort for reward.

Maybe you can imagine an army. Every soldier in the army knows his responsibilities because he has trained, practicing everything until it happens automatically, whenever an order is given. No soldiers stop to question their orders, because they trust their officers, so they proceed, as a team, competent in their skills and confident in their ability to get the task done. If any soldiers tried to avoid their tasks, the co-ordination of the whole army would fall apart, and their operation might fail.

So I'm sure you'd agree that strong guidance and a clear system is very useful for someone who would like to efficiently and effectively complete their tasks each day.

Maybe you had guidance like this even more recently, but now you don't, for whatever reason. Now you find yourself without someone else to jog you along, and keep you moving forwards. You're now having to take more responsibility for your own performance. You are the one who has to come up with the motivation each day.

Nothing has changed in your ability or capability. If you are finding things challenging, have no doubt that you can do what you set out to do. Your successes of the past, and there have been many, as you know, clearly demonstrate that you have what it takes, the personal resources you need.

The ability to self motivate is one of the most powerful attributes a person can have in their life. But nobody can tell you to throw your motivation switch and everything will be fine, because we both know that's not how it happens for you.

You respond well to a system, and you know that.

When you are organised with a clear plan, you are excellent at applying yourself and working methodically through your tasks. The plan keeps you focused. The plan prevents distractions, because the plan invites you to complete it quickly, so you can put it behind you. You always know what to do next.

Maybe now you miss having a plan.

Everyone needs a plan.

And deep inside you, where you know yourself best, you now understand that you could be everything you want to be, and achieve everything you want to achieve, by using a plan, and sticking to your plan.

Now, plans can be really simple, like the paper instructions you get with a flat pack table or wardrobe. See if you can imagine for a moment, this kind of plan. You know how it works, and it's very easy to follow:

First, there's a list of the parts, so that you make sure you can absolutely finish the project. People in warehouses all over he world have scurried round the shelves to collect all the parts that go into the package, and you can be confident when you check the list, that if you have all the parts, you will build the table successfully, because the next section of the plan guides you, move by move, to assemble the right pieces together. It's not complicated; it uses simple pictures which do not require you to question them, or to try and do things a different way.

The plan is progressive; you look at the picture, you find the parts, you put them together, and you move on to the next picture. All the while your table is changing from a pile of different parts, getting closer to the finished table, which is what you really want.

The result is the goal, and the process in between is simply the route you take to get there. If you follow the plan in sequence, you get a table. If you stop half way, or try to miss out some parts, you don't get a table. In fact, you get nothing.

It's a simple plan, designed to be the absolutely easiest and most effective way to build the table, step by step. And when you reach the end, and you look at your completed table, you feel great, because you successfully worked through a plan, and achieved the objective, in a lot less time than if you tried to work it out for yourself without a plan.

This plan is really just a list of tasks, things you need to do. It uses pictures to explain to people who do not speak the same language, so that they all get to a satisfactory result.

Plans you make only need to speak your language, so you don't need pictures. You can execute your plans very simply from lists of tasks that you write for yourself. You are the only one who knows what order your tasks will work best, to achieve your objective by the end of the day.

And here's the key; you'll have heard the phrase; 'early start, early finish' many time in your life. Well, it works, and here's the secret to early starting; be well organised. If you know exactly what it is you need to do, and you eliminate all uncertainty and distraction, there really is nothing stopping you from getting going each day. Nothing stopping you.

To be well organised, now we use our plan, which we already decided is a list of our tasks. A simple list of the things you need to do each day, in the order that they should be done. If you have that simple list, you can easily start early, and the list will enable you to maintain your focus and momentum throughout the day, so that you compete the tasks in an appropriate amount of time, and achieve your early finish.

Earlier we talked about modelling the habits of successful people, the way they behave which leads you to believe that you would like to be able to behave that way, to have those excellent habits of getting things done.

Well, a very important habit which these motivated people practice is to prepare their list in advance, usually the day before. At the end of each day, either their work day or before they settle down for the night, these successful, motivated people make their list ready for the next day. In a relaxed, quiet environment, these successful, motivated people find that they are able to think clearly about the tasks head, and set up their list correctly, knowing full well that they have a plan for the next day, which will give them the early start, early finish they enjoy most.

And from today forwards, your list is the most important habit that you adopt in your new way of doing things. You now take a few minutes at the end of each day, whilst your mind is still lively and energetic, to make your list for the next day. You don't take a long time over your list; you know exactly what needs to be done and you will be able to do each item and cross them off your list without hesitation or distraction, because your plan is clear.

And, deep inside yourself, you always knew that it could be this simple, to organise yourself according to a routine which works for successful, motivated people, as you have become a person like that, and you understand how to be at your best, and get things done when they need to be done.

And now, perhaps you'd like to take a moment permit the new knowledge you have acquired to filter permanently into your daily habits and routines. Imagine how it will be now that you have this new way of approaching your tasks and responsi-bilities.

You now prepare your list for the next day, because that is how successful people prepare.

You now sleep soundly each night, being certain that you are the best-organised version of yourself and you have a plan ready to go the very next day.

You start each new day with momentum, confident that your preparation has been thorough, and your task list will keep you focused and moving forwards as you complete each task and cross it off your list until there's nothing left.

You no longer feel the need to differentiate between tasks you like and tasks you don't. Each task has its own value, and you now benefit proportionally as you confidently complete each item on your list.

You now enjoy more freedom, more personal time, and more relaxation than before, because you have modelled the habits of successful, motivated people.

You may begin to find it hard to remember the way you were before, because you have now acquired a systematic way of maintaining your forward movement which is more satisfying and productive than that old you.

And you have achieved this wonderful change entirely by using your powerful subconscious mind, which knows what you need and desire, and is now equipped with the new behaviour patterns to enable you to achieve your fullest potential.

Please take as short moment of silence to relax even deeper and let your new knowledge firmly embed itself.

<<Pause>>

Well done. You've done so well.

Now in a moment I'm going to emerge you. You'll remember everything you've done and every place you've been....

EMERGE

You've done great. PAUSE. I'm going to count from ONE up to THREE. At the count of three your eyes are going to open, become fully alert, totally refreshed. Any cobwebs that you might have had, any sleepiness of mind is going to dissolve and disappear, and you're going to feel bright eyed and full of energy. You'll be fully alert and wonderful and marvellous in every way. ONE, slowly easily and gently feel yourself coming back up to your full awareness, At the count of TWO you're still relaxed and calm but notice that your eyes under your eyelids feel as if they're clearing, kind of like they're being bathed in a sparkling cool mountain stream, you feel GREAT. On the next count those eyes are going to open, totally alert, fully refreshed, just feeling excited, wonderful, in every way, and every time you go into hypnosis you can let yourself go deeper than the time before because you know that just feels good. All right, get ready, and on count of THREE open those eyes and notice how good you feel.

Session 2 Transcript

So, first check yourself to make sure you're absolutely ready to go into trance, and when you know it's time, take a slow, deep breath in, hold it for a second, close your eyes, and release it at your own speed.

As the breath flows out of you, feel your body begin to antici-pate how good it's going to feel to let yourself relax deeply as you've done before, and let your body relax, whilst you allow your breathing to find it's own, slow, steady rhythm, breathing in – and out – at exactly the correct speed for your body to take the nourishment it needs from each and every breath, and on your next breath in, I'd like to you to now open your eyes at the top of the breath, and then as you release the breath from your body, allow your eyes to close gently again. Good.

And now, as you breathe at your own speed, you feel your whole body begin to synchronise with your breathing, so that each time you breathe in you feel the life-giving air flowing through your whole body, and as you breathe out each time, you allow yourself to become even more deeply relaxed, feeling lazy and wonderful, and you know how good it will feel to go deeper so why not allow yourself to go all the way down now, as I start to count from ten down to one.

Ten – You are committed to finding a state of deep relaxation this time and every time you use hypnosis, and just this thought may be enough that you already begin to feel yourself more relaxed than a few moments before.

Nine – And so you have given yourself permission to do nothing else right now than allow the lazy, sensual feeling of releasing all the tension from your muscles and joints as you begin to settle into the journey to calmness and tranquillity

Eight – Deeper still, your body now so limp and floppy that you start to lose touch with your physical awareness, as you place your body in temporary hibernation – you won't be needing it for a little while, so allow it to rest

Seven – Move your attention to your face, and as you become aware of how your skin and tiny muscles of your face can easily be made to relax even more, and your face feels different now, and it's a wonderful, careless, lazy feeling as you completely release those muscles and just allow yourself to be

Six – Now your body and your face are totally relaxed and drifting safely, I'd like you to turn your attention back to your breathing and you can notice how this state of deep relaxation has slowed your breathing even more, and

Five – each time you breathe out, you naturally go deeper, as you've done before, and you possess knowledge about how effortlessly you can settle into this deepened state of consciousness, where you are the beneficiary of the personal power of change, and

Four – Now you begin to notice that your breathing is happening deeper in your body, lower down in your abdomen, and that kind of breathing feels good to you, and it is good, the best kind of breathing

Three – And now your body is at rest, and your breathing is happening at exactly the right speed, as you slowly drift down to that relaxed state that you've enjoyed so much so many times, and you know how good it feels

Two – As you start to notice that your descent is slowing as you reach the basement of your relaxation, and you may be curious about what will be the positive effect this time, and

One- You're there, totally relaxed, feeling wonderful, and you may now rest for a moment and settle into the gentle rhythm, aware of your regular, slow, controlled breathing, and allowing it to happen and your whole self to synchronise, and take a moment of silence to appreciate how you are right now...

<<Pause>>

Good, that's right.

Now that you have once more achieved this state of deep relaxation, listening only to the sound of my voice, and relaxing in rhythm with your breathing, you may begin to feel curious about what you will learn this time.

Before we get onto that, you have the opportunity to reflect on the progress you've made, and how that makes you feel. You have moved a long way from where you started, and the skills and techniques that you now possess may be some of the most useful things you'll learn in your life.

Perhaps you can begin to feel, somewhere deep inside, a tiny glow of satisfaction because you are now thinking and acting differently,

The Work

And now, combining all the knowledge you now possess, and the complete understanding and commitment that your new, motivated lifestyle is one of the most important decisions you ever made. In fact, it may be the most important decision, because its already clear to you that it's having a wonderful, refreshing effect on how you feel each day, both mentally and physically.

And you may even feel that making this change you have made is easier than you perhaps thought it would be, and maybe you sometimes wish that you made the change earlier, but that doesn't matter now, because you have made the change, and now you can use that to push yourself just a little more each day.

And even though you feel that it hasn't been difficult to make the change, its fair for us to agree that it isn't always easy to motivate yourself each day, even though you know that it's what you really want to do. Sometimes you may find yourself making a little excuse to delay something, maybe put it off until tomorrow, even though you know that you'll feel bad for the rest of the day.

That's OK to feel that way. It happens to everyone. Many people, in all walks of life, experience what you are experiencing, and many of them use a particular technique in order to overcome their inertia and move into their activities, and I'd like to show you how to do that now.

I'd like you to call on your powerful imagination now, and I'd like you to imagine you're preparing to run a sprint. Maybe you've run a race like this before, or maybe not, it doesn't matter, because I'm sure you've watched the Olympics on TV, so just allow your imagination to form an impression of yourself, in a stadium or just a school track, preparing to run.

You're already warmed up and you're waiting to be called to your marks.

See what you see, hear what you hear, feel what you feel.

Maybe you feel anticipation, excitement, or even nervousness about this race you're going to run. It must be important to you, because you've been training, but you have some tiny, nagging doubts about whether you're ready, whether you're capable of winning, whether you can stay the course to the finishing line.

And as you prepare yourself, you recall races like this that you've run before, even races you've won in the past, so you can focus on those races you ran before, and how good you felt when you won, or gave a good performance. All of the effort you put in comes back in a big rush at the end of the race.

But your nervousness grows; maybe you can feel it getting stronger somewhere in your body now, so try to locate that feeling and understand where it's coming from, and how it's affecting you.

If you allow that reluctance you are feeling now to grow too much, you might change your mind, and withdraw from the race.

Sure, that would be embarrassing, but at least you wouldn't have to risk failing. Because failing to you would be even more embarrassing than not starting in the first place.

Now you can experience the indecision for yourself. Stepping back is easy, but stepping forward is harder.

Now, holding those thoughts and feelings where they are right now, imagine you're looking down the track ahead of you, and focus on the finishing tape, which becomes clearer as you focus your attention. Crossing that tape will allow you to feel that rewarding feeling of accomplishment once again, as you have so many times before, and all you have to do is get there.

Now shift your attention to the ground directly in front of you, about a meter ahead. In your mind, draw a line across the ground, a white line, from left to right, a meter in front of you on the ground. Please do that now.

Now this line is very special. This line is called your line of commitment, and it's always there, every day, even though sometimes you forget to see it.

Your line of commitment is special because it only works one way. You can step over it from where you arE now, but you cannot step back from the other side; it simply won't allow you to step backwards.

On this side of your line of commitment, you are at rest. It might be relaxation, which you've earned and deserved, or it might be time when you're preparing, like warming up for this race you're preparing to run. While you're on this side of the line, you're stationary, not moving forwards or backwards.

You're getting ready.

Now, in a moment, but not just yet, you're going to step over the line, and when you do, you'll be in motion. Everything that happens to you after you take that step, everything you do to get yourself to the finish, from the way you set yourself in your starting blocks, to how you listen for the crack of the starter's pistol, throughout the race itself, when to push, when to cruise a little, is planned, because you've been preparing well and this is not your first race.

Go inside now and gather your energy and all the resources you need, and when you're sure that you've prepared yourself, take a longer breath than usual, and as you exhale it, step forward in your imagination, and cross your line of commitment.

And feel the change as you move from static to active, sense the forward motion, and notice how any doubts or misgivings you had are gone now, as you focus on moving forwards, making progress towards the finishing line, that goal you set for yourself, and where you know the good feelings of satisfaction and achievement will wait for you.

<<Pause>>

And you can now relax again, as you have proved your ability to discipline yourself in small and simple ways, and now you have your line of commitment, which you can create for yourself, any time you are facing tasks and challenges. Once you cross the line, you are active, and moving towards the finishing line.

And as you combine all of your skills and knowledge together, every day you feel stronger and more motivated than the day before, you have integrated your motivation as a permanent habit and behaviour.

You no longer have any need or desire to avoid or delay any activity.

Each day you actively seek out every opportunity to make progress, however small, because you know that each step forward takes you nearer to your life's goals.

You are easily able to push aside obstacles and excuses, and prioritise progress each day, because you have experienced the positive benefits your new habits bring to your life and those around you.

And I'm sure you'd agree with me that the new habits you've acquired are far more valuable than the old, unhelpful habits you have left behind, because you have now eliminated all trace of that, and you will never permit it to come back or yourself to behave in that old, out-dated way, because there is no need.

And I'd like to offer you generous portions of praise, and you can congratulate yourself on a job well done, and the changes you have made here today will stay with you from this day forwards, for the benefit of your whole life.

Good, very well done. Allow yourself to feel that pride for a few moments more.

<<Pause>>

Emerge

In a moment I'm going to count from ONE up to THREE. At the count of three your eyes are going to open, become fully alert, totally refreshed. Any sleepiness that you might have had, any dullness of mind is going to dissolve and disappear, and you're going to feel bright eyed and full of energy. You'll be fully alert and wonderful and marvellous in every way.

ONE, slowly easily and gently feel yourself coming back up to your full awareness,

At the count of TWO you're still relaxed and calm but notice that your eyes under your eyelids feel as if they're clearing, kind of like they're being bathed in a sparkling cool mountain stream, you feel GREAT.

On the next count those eyes are going to open, totally alert, fully refreshed, just feeling excited, wonderful, in every way, and every time you go into hypnosis you can let yourself go deeper than the time before because you know that just feels good.

All right, get ready, and on count of THREE open those eyes and notice how good you feel.

Session 3 Transcript

So, first check yourself to make sure you're absolutely ready to go into trance, and when you know it's time, take a slow, deep breath in, hold it for a second, close your eyes, and release it at your own speed.

As the breath flows out of you, feel your body begin to anticipate how good it's going to feel to let yourself relax deeply as you've done before, and let your body relax, whilst you allow your breathing to find it's own, slow, steady rhythm, breathing in – and out – at exactly the correct speed for your body to take the nourishment it needs from each and every breath, and on your next breath in, I'd like to you to now open your eyes at the top of the breath, and then as you release the breath from your body, allow your eyes to close gently again. Good.

And now, as you breathe at your own speed, you feel your whole body begin to synchronise with your breathing, so that each time you breathe in you feel the life-giving air flowing through your whole body, and as you breathe out each time, you allow yourself to become even more deeply relaxed, feeling lazy and wonderful, and you know how good it will feel to go deeper so why not allow yourself to go all the way down now, as I start to count from ten down to one.

Ten – You are committed to finding a state of deep relaxation this time and every time you use hypnosis, and just this thought may be enough that you already begin to feel yourself more relaxed than a few moments before.

Nine – And so you have given yourself permission to do nothing else right now than allow the lazy, sensual feeling of releasing all the tension from your muscles and joints as you begin to settle into the journey to calmness and tranquility

Eight – Deeper still, your body now so limp and floppy that you start to lose touch with your physical awareness, as you place your body in temporary hibernation – you won't be needing it for a little while, so allow it to rest

Seven – Move your attention to your face, and as you become aware of how your skin and tiny muscles of your face can easily be made to relax even more, and your face feels different now, and it's a wonderful, careless, lazy feeling as you completely release those muscles and just allow yourself to be

Six – Now your body and your face are totally relaxed and drifting safely, I'd like you to turn your attention back to your breathing and you can notice how this state of deep relaxation has slowed your breathing even more, and

Five – each time you breathe out, you naturally go deeper, as you've done before, and you possess knowledge about how effortlessly you can settle into this deepened state of conscious-ness, where you are the beneficiary of the personal power of change, and

Four — Now you begin to notice that your breathing is happening deeper in your body, lower down in your abdomen, and that kind of breathing feels good to you, and it is good, the best kind of breathing

Three — And now your body is at rest, and your breathing is happening at exactly the right speed, as you slowly drift down to that relaxed state that you've enjoyed so much so many times, and you know how good it feels

Two — As you start to notice that your descent is slowing as you reach the basement of your relaxation, and you may be curious about what will be the positive effect this time, and

One- You're there, totally relaxed, feeling wonderful, and you may now rest for a moment and settle into the gentle rhythm, aware of your regular, slow, controlled breathing, and allowing it to happen and your whole self to synchronise, and take a moment of silence to appreciate how you are right now...

<<pause>>

Good, that's right.

Now that you have once more achieved this state of deep relaxation, listening only to the sound of my voice, and relaxing in rhythm with your breathing, you may begin to feel curious about what you will learn this time.

Before we get onto that, you have the opportunity to reflect on the progress you've made, and how that makes you feel. You've traveled a long way from where you started. Now you have clear vision of your goals and objectives, and you plan each day, each month, each year, to give you a guide and schedule to get you to where you want to be.

The mental discipline that you're learning here may be one of the most useful things you'll add to your life.

Allow yourself to begin to feel, somewhere deep inside, a tiny glow of satisfaction, because you're now thinking and acting differently. You have understood and allowed yourself the capacity to make important changes, changes that will improve your happiness, your confidence, and your life.

The Work

You are equipped with all the tools, and you possess all the resources that a person needs to control how you respond and behave.

You are in charge of your own decisions: your thoughts and feelings are a part of you, you are not a part of them. You control your response to everyday challenges, they do not control you.

How you feel does not define you.

How you act defines you.

This is the way you have decided to live.

And you have also decided that your new life revolves around positive action, and that doing nothing is no longer something which serves you.

In a moment, I'd like you to think about a time when you allowed yourself to give in, weakly and with no resistance, to your emotional feelings, and didn't do something that now you wish you had.

Search for a time when you could have moved forwards and achieved something positive, but instead you allowed yourself to feel failure and regret.

Please go inside and find that time, as far back as you need. It's in your past, it cannot harm you, and it will begin to help you to identify those feelings that you had back then, and maybe you still have traces of, because if you had been motivated to take action, you might now be in a better place.

I will remain quiet for a short time, while you do that now.

<<pause>>

Well done.

Now, remembering that time, I'd like you to release any resistance in your body and just allow whatever feelings you had then, or you have now, to come to the surface, just for a moment.

Just continue to relax and let those feelings rise.

Now, you don't need to have these feelings any longer, but you do need to put them away somewhere where you will always know that they are there, but you'll make it hard for yourself to access them in the future.

Imagine now you're standing in front of two doors. The door on the left is dark grey, and it's cracked and worn, like it hasn't been painted for many years. The door on the right has glass panels and bright light behind it, and it looks new and clean. Both doors have locks, maybe like your front door at home. The keys are in the locks.

Be there now, see what you see, hear what you hear, and keep hold of those feelings of failure and inadequacy from that time before.

You know that you should choose a door to go through.

The door on the left, the old, worn, grey door, clearly isn't the one you like. You can't imagine anything good behind a door like that, can you?

The door on the right promises to lead you to a happy, comfortable, enjoyable future, which is the future you always wanted for yourself, and now here it is on offer.

Of course, you choose the door on the right, so you turn the key in the lock, and turn the handle, but the door will not open for you.

You try again, but the right-hand door will not open for you.

Step back for a moment, and think again.

The door on the right will not allow you through while you carry the negative feelings and emotions from before. The door on the right only allows people through who truly deserve to enjoy the satisfying results of making the effort to do better each day, to grow and thrive in the bright sunshine behind the right-hand door.

You need a way to get rid of the feelings you are carrying, the feelings that are entirely the fault of your emotional brain, the feelings that are preventing you from going through that door, into the sunshine.

So, try the key on the left-hand door, the grey door. Go on, try it now, and see how easily it turns in your hand, unlocking with a soft click. You turn the handle and slowly open the door.

You step inside and find yourself in a vast warehouse, with rows of high storage racks as far as you can see in all directions. These racks are stacked high with identical cardboard boxes, the same color grey as the door you just stepped through. There's a space in the rack right in front of you, the only space you can see, and there's a cardboard box on the floor.

Now, I'm sure you understand where you are and why you're here, so now, release those negative feelings you have carried for so long, those emotional restraints that used to hold you back and affect your motivation, and just allow those feelings to escape from you and fill up that cardboard box you have in front of you. Just let go every trace and morsel of those unwanted, unhelpful feelings, and let them flow into the box, until you are empty of those feelings and your box is full. Get it all out, now, because this is the only way it will work.

Go on, just release them completely.

Good.

Now close that box, that's right, and lift it up and slide it into the gap in the shelf.

Well done.

Step back through the grey door, and lock it behind you.

Take a moment to feel how free you've become. You've locked away the things you were not in control of, and they can't come back unless you unlock that door again, and take them out of the box.

And even if, from time to time, you may mistakenly think that there's some kind of reason to go and get back those feelings, you will remember how securely they are archived, and the reason why you placed them there, because they no longer serve you.

Now, try the right-hand door again, and see how smoothly and easily that key now turns. Open up the door, and allow the bright light to flood around you, drawing you into an energising, exciting place, where you know there's unlimited potential for those who have the courage to place their old ways and limitations behind the grey door. Go inside and find a feeling now, a feeling you welcome, a feeling that you can allow to grow, to move and spin inside you. Let it build, and feel those tiny electric waves of pleasure start to trickle through you.

This is the reward for your strength. This is the way you're allowing yourself to feel, now that you took control your actions, and banished your emotional restrictions behind the grey door.

And from this day forwards, each and every time that you open a door, anywhere, anytime, you'll be reminded of the moment when you consigned your past habits and behaviours behind a grey door which you need never open again.

And each and every time you walk through a door you have opened, you can allow yourself to feel a small wave of this positive, energetic reward that you are enjoying, because every door you walk through is a move in a positive direction, a step taken with courage and optimism, with curiosity and anticipation.

You approach each day with strength and courage, because you understand the rewards available to you for positive, motivated, action.

You push down any negative emotional signals, that you might have listened to in the past, because you know it's a trick to stop you, or slow you down, and you don't fall for tricks like that.

You take complete enjoyment and satisfaction from the way you now see yourself, as that person who doesn't step back, but always pushed forwards with energy and conviction.

And you grow each day, as you find it easy and automatic to move at the speed you always wanted to, finishing and closing everything you start in plenty of time to allow you to rest.

So, let these new, useful, automatic habits and responses filter through your mind, and find their correct place, where they can permanently rewrite your old ways, because those old habits no longer serve you.

Take a few moments of silence to do that now.

<<pause>>

Emerge

You've done great. PAUSE. I'm going to count from ONE up to THREE. At the count of three your eyes are going to open, become fully alert, totally refreshed. Any cobwebs that you might have had, any sleepiness of mind is going to dissolve and disappear, and you're going to feel bright eyed and full of energy.

You'll be fully alert and wonderful and marvellous in every way. ONE, slowly easily and gently feel yourself coming back up to your full awareness, At the count of TWO you're still relaxed and calm but notice that your eyes under your eyelids feel as if they're clearing, kind of like they're being bathed in a sparkling cool mountain stream, you feel GREAT. On the next count those eyes are going to open, totally alert, fully refreshed, just feeling excited, wonderful, in every way, and every time you go into hypnosis you can let yourself go deeper than the time before because you know that just feels good.

All right, get ready, and on the count of THREE open those eyes and notice how good you feel.

PROGRAM DEBRIEF

CONGRATULATIONS! You've now completed *The Motivation Code* program.

We've covered a great deal of ground and you've been exposed to several angles of attack, of which one or all are bound to have an ongoing positive effect, so long as you use them regularly.

Revisit these recordings often. Repeating them will continue to strengthen your new automatic behaviour, and there really is no limit to how much you can achieve.

I wish you luck and good fortune in whatever you choose to do with it.

OTHER RICK SMITH PROGRAMS & BOOKS

If you've enjoyed *The Motivation Code,* here are some other programs which might interest you:

What's Holding You Back?

• Maybe you're struggling with social situations? Wanting to start new friendships, but wary of putting yourself out there.

• Perhaps you want to be more confident in your work life? You've seen how more assertive people progress and succeed, and you'd like to be able to do that for yourself.

• Or are you facing presentation or performance anxiety?

You have a great story to tell, but you're held back, anxious about the things that could go wrong, and ignoring the - more likely - outcome that everything goes right?

Is Shyness Stopping You Living The Life You Want?

Many people suffer all their lives, and never act. Their philosophy? If you never try, you'll never fail.

But if you never take a risk, you'll never feel the elation of a well-earned reward.

Let's Make A Change!

In **Cool, Calm, Confident You**, you'll be re-discovering strengths you've unwittingly suppressed or buried, and learning how to put them together and make them work for you.

These hypnosis tools will empower you to modify your emotional responses and remove your unnecessary obstructions to living a fuller, more confident life.

Once you've understood the rewards, you'll be highly motivated to learn and practice the methods of obtaining them.

By the time you complete the three sessions, repeating

them as necessary, you'll have acquired all the tools and techniques you need to face any situation with calmness, and confidence in your ability to deal with any challenge.

Explore on ricksmithhypnosis.com

Stress - Take Control and Crush It, Now.

You know what it's like. That old familiar feeling starts to trouble you; it grows and mutates, sucking your energy, attention, and logical thought into a ball of aching tension, clouding your judgment and influencing your actions.

It starts in your head, but it invades your whole body, and you hate it.

Time for action...

You're Not Alone - You Can Fix Yourself

Chronic or ongoing stress can wreak havoc on your body, significantly raising your risk of serious illness. Scientists now consider underlying stress to be one of the top-three hidden killers.

The main culprit is *cortisol,* a naturally occurring, usually benign steroid hormone, which regulates many of your body's important functions. But when uncontrolled cortisol is allowed to flood your body, the damage is serious, and cumulative.

Once you understand what's happening, it's not that difficult to adapt your response so that the cortisol effects are suppressed, and you remain stable and grounded without losing your focus.

Using hypnosis, you'll learn to equalise before cortisol scores: simple techniques and routines that will enable you to remain cool and calm in the face of your challenges and navigate yourself - and those around you - through those difficult times.

By the time you complete the three sessions, repeating them as necessary, you'll have acquired all the tools and techniques you need to face any situation with calmness, and confidence in your ability to deal with any challenge.

And you'll feel a whole lot better than you do right now!

Explore on ricksmithhypnosis.com

Anxiety - you feel it rising, so take control and crush it, now.

You know what it's like. That old familiar feeling starts to trouble you; it grows and mutates, sucking your energy, attention, and logical thought into a ball of aching tension, clouding your judgment and influencing your actions. You hate it, and it never helps. Whatever you've tried hasn't worked, so you're looking for something different.

You're not alone - you can fix yourself

Anxiety comes in many forms, but it's usually caused by fear of something that you think is about to happen, and the way that it's going to make you feel. Your imagination perceives an impending threat and fires off a salvo of chemicals into your brain and bloodstream to alert you. Many people suffer all their lives, and never acknowledge that they need help to get on top of the condition.

Yet, once you understand what's happening, it's not that difficult to adapt your response so that the effects of these chemicals are suppressed, and you get back to normal quickly without losing your focus. Using hypnosis, you'll learn to separate your thoughts and feelings when anxiety approaches, and to focus on the outcome, not the process. You'll be able to remain cool and calm in the face of your challenges, and navigate yourself, and those around you, through those difficult situations.

By the time you complete the three sessions, repeating them as necessary, you'll have acquired all the tools and techniques you need to face any situation with calmness, and confidence in your ability to deal with any challenge.

And you'll feel a whole lot better than you do right now!

Explore on ricksmithhypnosis.com

Why Are You Still Putting Things Off?

Procrastination - You hate it, and it never helps. How come other people seem to get things done? You know what it's like. You've things to do but you're finding every possible reason to avoid getting started.

Why does it always have to be this way?

You're Not Alone

Many people suffer all their lives, and never acknowledge that they need help to get on top of the bad habits and anxiety that comes with putting things off.

• Maybe you're a perfectionist? You don't want to start something because you're fearful of your ability to complete it to your own high standards, even though you may have done it – successfully - many times before.

• Or perhaps you feel inadequate or unworthy? You think – usually wrongly – that you're going to fail, so you'd rather not take the risk. Even though you know this is an illogical mind-set.

• Or is it simply that you hate the things you have to do, so you find any reason to avoid doing them? Until you absolutely have to!

You feel trapped, a hostage to procrastination.

It Doesn't Have To Be This Way

In these hypnosis sessions, we'll approach the challenge from all sides. Each recording is progressive: you'll learn and practice something and then carry that skill forwards to the next session.

By the time you complete the three sessions, you'll have

mastered the capability to remain fully focused and highly motivated in every situation, knowing full well that the rewards of powering ahead are many times greater than those of holding back.

Explore on ricksmithhypnosis.com

ricksmithhypnosis.com

AFTERWORD

The Scripts Used in this Book

The recordings we used in this program can be streamed or downloaded free once you register at

http://tiny.cc/amzmotv

If you encounter any issues obtaining the recordings, please e-mail me and I'll fix it for you.

rick@ricksmithhypnosis.com

If you enjoy the book and you find something worthwhile in the system, please take a moment to post a Review on Amazon.

However you decide to use your new skills, above all - *enjoy the journey!*

Rick Smith

Made in the USA
Monee, IL
03 September 2021